INFLUENTIAL ECONOMISTS

PROFILES

INFLUENTIAL ECONOMISTS

Marie Bussing-Burks

The Oliver Press, Inc.
Minneapolis

To Barry, Annemarie, and Katie

The Oliver Press, Inc.
Charlotte Square
5707 West 36th Street
Minneapolis, MN 55416-2510

Library of Congress Cataloging-in-Publication Data

Bussing-Burks, Marie, 1958-
   Influential economists / Marie Bussing-Burks.
      p. cm. — (Profiles ; 32)
   Summary: Presents information on the lives and work of the
economists Thomas Gresham, Adam Smith, Thomas Robert
Malthus, Karl Marx, John Maynard Keynes, Milton Friedman,
and Alan Greenspan.
   Includes bibliographical references and index.
   ISBN 1-881508-72-2
   1. Economists—Biography—Juvenile literature.
[1. Economists.] I. Title. II. Profiles (Minneapolis, Minn.) ; 32.

HB76 .B87 2003
330'.092'2—dc21
[B]
                                                 2001059310

ISBN 1-881508-72-2
Printed in the United States of America
09 08 07 06 05 04 03   8 7 6 5 4 3 2 1

Contents

A United States Treasury clerk counts money inside a vault in about 1907. Helping people and governments make decisions about how to spend their money is one of the major concerns of many economists.

Introduction

Who was routinely dubbed the second most powerful person in the United States in the 1990s, right behind the president? A politician, a banker, a lawyer? No—none other than an economist, Federal Reserve Chairman Alan Greenspan. As leader of the nation's central bank, Greenspan guided the U.S. economy through a period of spectacular growth while working to reduce unemployment and control inflation. Along the way, he became the most famous economist of his time. But economists have been influencing the course of world events for hundreds of years, even before there was a name for what they did.

Economists study the way in which individuals and societies use their resources to produce, distribute, and consume goods and services. Because resources are limited, all needs and desires cannot be met at once. Every person, corporation, and government must make economic decisions. Individuals might deal with issues as simple as whether to save their money or spend it on a new CD. Nations, meanwhile, could face the choice between using more tax dollars for national defense or spending more on education. Economists try to predict how these decisions will be made and which choices are most likely to create a strong, functioning economy that gives as many people as possible access to the material things they want and need.

People have struggled with economic problems since the beginning of history. Early communities spent nearly all their time obtaining food, tools, and shelter. Their economic decisions were basic: whether to spend the day hunting or gathering plants for their dinner, how to divide food among tribe members, and where to build their huts. They had little time for any concerns beyond survival. It would be centuries before human societies were sophisticated enough to deliberately consider their economic choices in an effort to improve their standard of living.

Some of the first recorded individuals to make observations about economics lived during the fourth century B.C. in Greece. At that time, the Greek economy revolved around agriculture and relied on slave labor for most of its farming and crafts, but it was also becoming more dependent on trade. The Greeks exported grains, grapes, olives, timber, jewels, spices, and pottery to their trading partners in the empires around the Mediterranean

Sea. In return, they received important materials such as clay, marble, iron, and silver. Although bartering (exchanging goods for other goods) was still common, the Greeks had begun using money in the form of metal coins, which were more easily accepted in the unfamiliar lands in which they traded.

With commerce booming, Greek philosophers tried to develop guidelines about how people should work and earn wealth. Plato (427-347 B.C.) believed that in an ideal society, workers would happily perform the duties for which they were suited. Employing people according to what they did best would result in greater production with less labor. Feeling that any pursuit of private profit—such as that practiced by the traders—would cause discontent in society, Plato called for common owner-ship of property so that all people could share equally in the wealth. He abandoned this idea in later works, how-ever, noting that people could not easily manage their affairs together.

Plato's student Aristotle (384-322 B.C.) was also sus-picious of the wealth generated by trade. He believed that money was not a natural form of wealth, only a conve-nient tool for people to use in exchange. Real wealth came from agriculture, in which labor was applied to raw materials to produce food and other goods. Aristotle believed agricultural work was the only honorable job; the occupations of trader, craftsman, and laborer were undignified and should be reserved for foreigners and

Aristotle wrote about nearly every subject, including logic, ethics, politics, poetry, biology, and physics. Most of his published writings have been lost, and his ideas are mainly known through student lecture notes and textbooks from the Lyceum, the school he founded in Athens.

slaves. He knew that trade was beneficial in obtaining many necessities, but he believed it encouraged people to accumulate wealth for wealth's sake. He also disapproved of charging interest on loans, believing it promoted unnatural wealth and economic inequality.

Although economic conditions changed over the following centuries, economic thought advanced little. It was not until the Middle Ages that another European recorded significant observations about trade and wealth. By that time, Christianity had become nearly universal throughout Europe. Since Christian doctrine frowned on personal gain, few working people sought profits for themselves. European economies were based on a system called feudalism, in which land was controlled by wealthy landlords and farmed by laborers known as serfs. Rather than being sold in trade, most agricultural products were distributed among the people. Serfs had to turn over as much as half of each harvest to their landlord, keeping the rest for their own provisions. Goods were made by craftsmen, whose work was modestly paid and regulated by guilds (an early form of today's trade unions).

The great economic thinker of the feudal era was Thomas Aquinas (1225-1274), a scholar who blended the interests of both business and religion. He was a monk, and his main concern was with issues of justice and morality. But Aquinas also understood the importance of trade; he came from northern Italy, a region where trade flourished. Although he shared many of Aristotle's viewpoints, Aquinas was more supportive of commerce. He opposed charging interest on loans, but he said interest charges were acceptable in certain circumstances (for example, if repayment was delayed). Instead of condemning wealth, Aquinas believed that in itself it was neither good nor bad—but it could be put to good or bad use. His ideas helped to justify increased economic activity.

Economic theories were only a minor part of the work of early philosophers like Plato, Aristotle, and Aquinas, and they did not provide many practical suggestions about how to conduct business. It was not until commerce became more acceptable and widespread that economists would emerge. In the fifteenth century, the economy of Western Europe changed from feudalism to mercantilism, a system in which the state controlled economic activity. Most nations were ruled by monarchs who supported armies for defense, paid employees to keep the government running smoothly, and collected taxes to meet expenses. The monarchs encouraged and protected business activity because it resulted in more tax revenues for them. They financed exploration and trade ventures abroad, such as Christopher Columbus's four voyages across the Atlantic (sponsored by Queen Isabella and King Ferdinand of Spain). Expanded overseas trade dissolved the feudal system of sharing goods and brought wealth and power to the merchants who bought, sold, and

One English merchant's bustling business in about 1550. Traders negotiate deals while employees weigh and store goods and record transactions.

shipped goods all over the world. *Influential Economists* begins during this time with the story of one such merchant, Sir Thomas Gresham. Although he would not have called himself an economist, Gresham saved three English monarchs from bankruptcy, amassed great wealth for himself and his country, and formulated one of the earliest economic laws.

The study of economics was not truly born until the 1700s. By then, the mercantilist view of gold and silver as wealth was beginning to look too shallow. A series of technological breakthroughs known as the Industrial Revolution changed the way that goods were produced, starting in the mid-1700s in England and spreading through the United States and Europe in the next century. Handcrafted goods were replaced by machine-made, mass-produced factory products. Scottish economist Adam Smith believed that this increased manufacturing represented greater wealth for society. Theorizing that the forces of supply and demand coordinate economic activity, he argued for more competition and less government involvement in the economy. Smith became known as the first and greatest proponent of capitalism, the system of private property and individual action that is the basis for the modern world economy.

By the mid-1800s, English industry was booming and productivity was soaring, but not everyone seemed to be benefiting. Dangerous conditions, long workdays, monotonous tasks, and paltry wages all contributed to a

A steam hammer in an iron foundry in 1850. Harnessing the power of steam to run machines was one of the most important advances of the Industrial Revolution. The many factories and smokestacks visible through the open door testify to the rapid growth of industry during this time.

harsh life for many factory workers. Troubled by the misery they saw in industrial towns, some economists sought ways to distribute wealth more equitably among society's members. Thomas Robert Malthus, a clergyman who became England's first professor of economics, dismally predicted that population was increasing faster than the supply of food. Foreseeing mass starvation unless population growth could be controlled, Malthus brought to light issues of poverty and sustainable growth that are

14

still debated today. The best-known critic of capitalism, however, was Karl Marx, a radical German philosopher and political activist. He believed capitalism had serious flaws that would eventually cause it to collapse. The poorly paid and overworked laborers would revolt and institute a new system: communism, a classless society with no private property. Marx's theories launched a worldwide communist movement that led to revolutions in Russia, China, and other countries.

Despite these dissenting voices, classical economists inspired by Adam Smith ruled economics until the early twentieth century. They believed in a natural business cycle in which economic conditions corrected themselves without government intervention. But when the 1929 stock market crash launched the longest depression the capitalist world had ever seen, many people feared that the economy would not correct itself. They believed some drastic action was needed, and British economist John Maynard Keynes had an answer. Keynes suggested that the government should step in and spend money to get the economy moving again. His ideas won many sup-porters when U.S. President Franklin Roosevelt's New Deal programs and massive defense spending during World War II helped end the Great Depression. Keynes's impact was felt around the world. His theories dominated mainstream economics until the early 1970s and are still employed by governments today.

When another economic crisis struck in the early 1970s, with a slowing U.S. economy and prices rising out of control, a very different economist stepped in with a very different solution. University of Chicago professor Milton Friedman studied money and its effect on the economy. Directly opposing Keynesian theory, he suggested that the supply of money, rather than government spending programs, was the most important factor in the economy. Implemented by the Federal Reserve Bank between 1979 and 1982, his controversial ideas helped end a serious inflation problem and inspired a school of economics called monetarism.

Even as many economists still advocated monetarism, the government and the public continued to search for different solutions to the country's economic ills. The U.S. economy endured two tough recessions in the early 1980s and a brief recession in 1991. But through the rest of the 1990s, it enjoyed the strongest expansion phase in American history. Many people credited this success to Federal Reserve Chairman Alan Greenspan, who took office in 1987. Rather than controlling the money supply directly, as the monetarists suggested, Greenspan actively adjusted interest rates to maintain a strong economy. Because the U.S. is the world's largest producer of goods and services, the actions of this economist were watched around the globe.

Greenspan's fame mirrors the increased success of economics as a field of study. As economic systems grow more complex, the work of economists has expanded and gained prominence. Today, more economists than ever before are forming theories to guide people's economic decisions. Some, in positions of political power, apply policies designed to help their nations achieve a higher standard of living. Others work for corporations, helping them to increase their profits. Still other economists teach and write to help individuals better understand the complex personal, business, and government choices that can stimulate or slow down economic growth, encourage or stifle employment opportunities, and raise or lower prices.

Economies now produce millions, billions, and even trillions of dollars in new goods and services each year. The U.S. leads annual production at about $10 trillion, followed by Japan at nearly $5 trillion and Germany at just under $2 trillion. But producers in the billions, such as Canada, Mexico, and Sweden, are also forceful players. And smaller producers—Tonga at $153 million, for example—participate in the global economy, too. As the world becomes increasingly interconnected through trade, the theories of influential economists affect all countries, small and large, for better or worse. At their best, they may help more people gain the opportunity to work, produce goods and services, and buy the things they want and need.

As a merchant, banker, and royal adviser, Sir Thomas Gresham (1519-1579) wielded great financial power and formulated some of the earliest economic principles.

1

Thomas Gresham
Royal Financial Agent

*I*n the fifteenth and sixteenth centuries, the European economy was transformed by a "commercial revolution." Advancements in sea travel helped explorers voyage to Africa, Asia, and North and South America, where they discovered new resources and opened up new markets for trade. Increasingly, European nations collected wealth—which at the time was measured in gold and silver—through international commerce. Monarchs strictly controlled economic activity and increased exports to accumulate more cash, a system known as mercantilism.

Mercantilist policy was meant to benefit the nation as a whole, but one group benefited most—the merchants, a new middle class created by the rise of international trade. Merchants exported goods from their own countries and imported other items from abroad, often reselling them at a significant profit. The wealthiest merchants owned their own ships, while others rented them for their voyages overseas. Those with extra funds sometimes acted as moneylenders, making loans to others and earning a profit by charging interest. Merchants held one of the most profitable, powerful, and adventurous jobs available. They gambled their fortunes on daring business transactions. At a time when travel was rare and often hazardous, they traversed the world, always in danger from pirates who might storm their ships, seize their merchandise, and kill the entire crew. But while the risks were high, the rewards were even greater.

Thomas Gresham was destined for a merchant's life. His father, two of his uncles, and his older brother won status and wealth in the trading business. But it was Thomas who would bring fame to an already respected family name. His success as a merchant earned him the job of royal financial agent to three English monarchs. In this powerful position, he was instrumental in his country's economic survival, helping England to amass gold and silver, repay its debts, and issue a stable currency. Centuries before economics became a recognized area of study, Thomas Gresham managed to develop practical theories about how financial decisions could affect a nation's welfare.

Thomas was born in London, likely in the year 1519, to Audrey Lynne Gresham and Richard Gresham. He had an older brother, John, and two sisters, Elizabeth and Christiana. The Greshams lived happily and comfortably in a spacious home on Milk Street, in the heart of London's trading district. Richard Gresham was a successful cloth merchant growing wealthier every day, and he served for a time as lord mayor of London. All was rosy for the family until tragedy struck: when Thomas was a mere three years old, his mother died of a mysterious fever. Although grief-stricken, his father remarried. Richard's new wife was a wealthy young widow, Isabella Taverson. Isabella capably managed the family's three homes and supervised a staff of servants, nannies, and tutors. In addition, she reared all four Gresham children with attention, love, and care. Thomas quickly grew to love Isabella as a mother.

Thomas was schooled at home by tutors who taught him history, philosophy, and religion. Although he was a diligent student, his father's work interested him more. As in all tradesmen's houses at the time, the bottom floor of the Gresham home served as a shop where Richard conducted business. It was a stimulating environment for bright, curious young Thomas. He listened astutely to his father's stories of sailing to other countries, and he feverishly studied the maps his father used to plot courses for his ships. From an early age, Thomas dreamed of discovering new lands and riches for England.

Richard Gresham wanted to be sure his son had a formal education before entering the family business, so he sent Thomas to Gonville College at Cambridge University in 1531. Four years later, at age 16, Thomas left school and began working as an apprentice to his merchant uncle, Sir John Gresham, learning to negotiate shrewdly with other traders. At 24, he was admitted as a member of the Mercers' Company, officially beginning his career as a merchant. Deriving its name from the French word for "merchant," the Mercers' Company was

The first page of Thomas Gresham's personal account book, which he began in 1546, soon after becoming a merchant. This elaborate, meticulous book demonstrates the care with which he organized his finances.

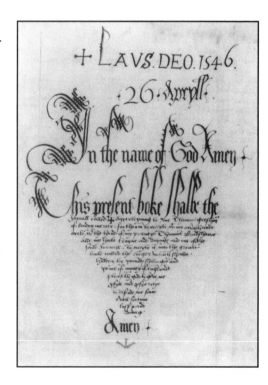

London's premier guild—an organization of merchants who grouped together to protect themselves from competition. They paid the crown for a charter, which gave them the right to control the import and export of their goods and restrict the number of merchants admitted into the guild. Joining a guild was a great privilege, for it was the only way merchants could gain the right to trade certain types of merchandise. The Mercers' Company allowed members to deal in England's chief commodities: wool, silk, cotton, and other woven goods.

In 1551, Thomas Gresham was appointed as King Edward VI's royal financial agent at Antwerp, the Belgian city that was the commercial center of Europe. There, merchants from many countries would gather to make loans, collect interest, and exchange goods. This could often be a complex process, since there was no common currency. Countries, regions, and even some cities had their own coins, different from others in name and value. Gresham had noticed early in his career that the value of one currency in relation to other currencies—the exchange rate—was a critical factor in business, as well as in a nation's economy. Merchants could gain or lose money in transactions depending on the exchange rate. Gresham's job in Antwerp would be to buy supplies for England's army and to negotiate the king's loans at the best rates possible.

England was anything but poverty-stricken; it profitably exported wool and woolen cloth. The problem

Soldiers and merchants board a ship in Antwerp harbor in 1578. The comings and goings of people—especially traders—from around the world made Antwerp the busiest port in Europe.

was that the government was always borrowing money. The royalty liked to live well and wage expensive wars of conquest, but they knew that raising the taxes on their people above a certain level was not wise. They had to find the money elsewhere to support their spending, so they borrowed heavily from Flemish, German, and Italian moneylenders, who often charged high rates of interest. Around 1550, the annual interest owed by King Edward was 40,000 pounds—a tremendous amount of money at the time. As royal financial agent, Gresham was continually looking for credit from the moneylenders of Europe and always having to put off repayment of the loans. So he decided the king needed a payment plan. He suggested Edward set aside money each week to pay off his debts, and in two years he would be out of debt.

Edward initially stuck with the plan, sending Gresham 1,200 pounds a week for eight weeks. But the payments stopped when some of Edward's advisers decided the exchange rates were not favorable to England. To raise the relative value of English money and make it easier for the king to pay back his debts, Gresham took steps to control the exchange rate. He urged England to keep as much gold and silver as possible within the country, limiting the supply abroad and thus making it more valuable.

Gresham also forced English wool merchants to loan money to Edward. He detained their ships as they were about to set sail to sell goods abroad, refusing to let them leave until they agreed to lend the money. Even though they were promptly repaid upon their return to England, this move did not win Gresham favor among the merchants. It did, however, accomplish his goal of repaying England's foreign debts, though Edward was never as prompt with his payments as Gresham would have liked.

Edward was pleased with Gresham's financial dealings, but the act that delighted the king the most was a simple gift. In 1552, Gresham gave Edward some long Spanish silk stockings as a New Year's present. Enamored

The only son of King Henry VIII, Edward VI (1537-1553) became king at the age of 10, although advisers such as his uncle, the duke of Somerset, held most of the real power during his reign.

with the stockings, the king rewarded Gresham with some property in June 1553. As Edward handed over the charter to the land, he said, "You shall know that you have served a king." A few weeks later, Edward, a mere 16 years old, died from tuberculosis. His half-sister Mary succeeded him.

Queen Mary reappointed Gresham as royal financial agent in Antwerp. She then ordered him to borrow 50,000 pounds in gold or silver and ship it to England. Although Gresham had helped to build up England's credit under King Edward, borrowing from other countries was still difficult because of competitive and often hostile feelings between nations, none of which wanted to lose valuable gold and silver to its rivals. In many places, including Antwerp, shipping large amounts of coin out of the country was against the law. Gresham would risk imprisonment if he were captured, but he had no choice except to obey the queen, so he undertook the challenge with gusto. He negotiated 50,000 pounds in loans from bankers, largely in silver coins, and then plotted how to smuggle the money out of Antwerp.

His first plan called for hiding some silver coins in each bag of a large shipment of pepper. But he would have to buy massive quantities of expensive pepper to hide all the coins, and he feared that the silver would add obvious weight to the bags. He abandoned this scheme, deciding instead to buy weapons and armor and hide some coins in every shipping container. Military equipment was more necessary to England than pepper, and a large shipment of it would seem less suspicious. To ensure his plan's success, Gresham became friendly with the Antwerp custom-house officers, whose job it was to regulate and inspect what entered or left the country. He gave every custom-house officer gifts of cloth for New Year's, and they looked the other way on his dealings. Gresham succeeded in sneaking all 50,000 pounds out of Antwerp without any search or questioning. As thanks for this elaborate undertaking, he received a royal document addressed to Her Majesty's "trusty and well-beloved servant, Thomas Gresham, Esquire."

Upon Gresham's return from Antwerp in 1554, Mary dispatched him on a mission to Spain. She wanted him to convert bills of exchange (written orders for a specified sum, often used to transfer money internationally) into a share of the immense gold and silver treasure Spain had gained from its conquest of Mexico and Peru. Gresham traded the bills for gold, even managing to bring in a profit by playing on favorable exchange rates. But Spain had strict laws to keep its gold and silver within the country, and even the daring adventurer felt it was too risky to smuggle coin out of well-policed Spain. Gresham decided to take the safe route, calling on the queen's powerful soon-to-be relatives. Since Mary was to wed Prince Philip of Spain that year, Gresham asked Philip's

A devout Catholic in a newly Protestant nation, Mary I (1516-1558) had a stormy reign. Her marriage to Philip of Spain (also a Catholic) was unpopular, and the persecution of Protestants during her rule earned her the nickname "Bloody Mary."

mother, the queen of Spain, for help. She, however, was not happy to see so much gold leave the country, even if it was for her son's new wife. Negotiations were much more difficult than Gresham could have imagined, and the process of procuring a passport for the money took him several months. Eventually, though, he succeeded—in the same month that Mary and Philip were married.

Queen Mary died in 1558 and was succeeded by her half-sister, Elizabeth. By this time, the economic situation in England had once again deteriorated. Wars waged by Philip had raised the national debt to 227,000 pounds a year; Elizabeth would need the astronomical sum of 300,000 pounds just to cover her immediate financial needs. Gresham, reappointed as royal agent, seized this opportunity to influence the queen's policies. In a long letter to Elizabeth, Gresham thoroughly summarized England's recent economic history, analyzing the decisions that had been made by previous rulers and how they had affected the nation. He then gave the queen some basic advice: accumulate as little foreign debt as possible and keep England's credit good. The queen followed his suggestions. She paid off her debts and avoided incurring new ones by reducing the court's expenses. The annual debt was eventually brought down to 17,000 pounds, the lowest it had been in nearly 100 years.

Gresham pointed out to Elizabeth that years earlier, the government of her father, King Henry VIII, had begun reducing the gold content of English coins. As a

Elizabeth I (1533-1603) was an influential ruler who presided over a period of great cultural development. Art and literature thrived, voyages of exploration increased, and England began to emerge as a world power.

result, some of the coins circulating in England were made of gold mixed with less valuable metals, while older coins were of pure gold. Both were worth the same amount at face value, but the coins with more gold in them had more value if melted down and sold as pure metal. Since wealth at the time was measured in gold and silver, the coins with the most gold content had the most worth in the international market. Gresham believed that the "good" gold English coins were being hoarded or used to settle debts abroad, while the coins spent within England were the ones with less gold in them. The nation was thus losing a great deal of its valuable metal. He suggested the queen issue a new currency that contained a standard amount of precious metal, and she wisely did so. The more stable currency made traders from other countries more interested in entering into long-term financial agreements based upon English coin, which increased the nation's wealth.

Gresham's advice to Queen Elizabeth secured his place in economic history. Although he was not the first to express the principle that bad money will drive good money out of circulation, the idea became known as Gresham's Law. It has proved true throughout the centuries and is still commonly accepted today. The modern definition of wealth is far more complex than the accumulation of gold and silver, and most governments have withdrawn the valuable metal from their coins, replacing it with copper, zinc, and nickel. When this happened, people spent the new coins, collecting and hoarding the old ones until they were no longer in circulation—just as Gresham's Law predicted.

Thomas Gresham's home life initially seemed to be as successful as his business dealings. In 1544, he had married widow Anne Ferneley Read. Anne's late husband, William Read, had been a friend of Thomas's father, Richard. When Richard had learned William was ill, he had asked his son to ride to Suffolk to check on the family. Thomas ended up visiting Suffolk many times, and he and Anne became fast friends. The dying William Read noticed the attraction, and he suggested to Richard that Thomas and Anne marry upon his death. The couple settled in London, and about a year later, Anne gave

Painted to celebrate Thomas Gresham's wedding in 1544, this portrait of the handsome, prosperous 26-year-old merchant is inscribed with the couple's initials: "A. G. love, serve and obei [obey] T. G."

birth to a baby boy. They named their son Richard, after his grandfather.

The marriage was strong at first, but Anne was not happy after they settled in Antwerp in 1551. She felt like a stranger in Belgium and could not speak the language. Thomas was immersed in the crown's business and was not at home much. As the marriage deteriorated, Thomas began a relationship with a woman who lived in nearby Bruges. The woman eventually gave birth to a daughter, whom Thomas named Marie-Anne. Just one month after the baby was born, the mother died. Thomas brought the child home, and Anne selflessly raised her as her own—calling her Anne, after herself. Thomas and his wife remained married, although there were times when they rarely spoke to each other.

While conducting business for the crown, Thomas still ran his own successful merchant trade, amassing a great private fortune through importing and exporting goods, owning ships, and lending money. He planned for his son, Richard, to take over the company when he retired. But in 1564, when Richard was just 20 years old, he died when a fever struck the trading ship he was aboard. Thomas, who had placed all his hopes for the future in Richard's hands, was devastated. On a cold, wintry day, he and Anne buried their only son at St. Helen's Church, near their home in London.

Queen Elizabeth knighted Thomas Gresham in 1559 for his years of faithful service to the crown. This knighthood, the same honor that had been bestowed on his father, his uncle, and his older brother, fulfilled his life-long dream. Gresham was proud of the recognition, and he delighted to see England thriving under his economic policies. He was concerned, however, by the fact that London had no proper meeting place for merchants to trade or make loans. Businessmen commonly negotiated their deals at the side of the road, often in the rain, like vagrants. Gresham knew the other European trading centers had organized a physical location for such activities. His father had wanted such a place when he was sheriff of London, but he had not won the public support needed for the project.

Feeling a strong sense of duty to see his father's wishes realized, Sir Thomas Gresham became determined to found a center for trade. His resolution only increased when his son died, leaving him without an heir to carry on his name and fortune. After eight years of work, Gresham completed his legacy: the Royal Exchange. Formally dedicated by the queen in 1571, the Royal Exchange was a building where merchants could meet daily, trade their goods, and negotiate loans. By Elizabeth's death in 1603, the exchange had helped build London into the financial capital of all of Europe.

The founder of this great institution, the successful merchant and great economist, died suddenly, likely of a stroke, on November 21, 1579, at the age of 60. Queen Elizabeth wept openly when informed of his death, and she sent her guards to preside over the funeral procession. In a ceremony filled with the splendor and pageantry fit for nobility, Sir Thomas Gresham was buried next to his son in St. Helen's Church.

As Gresham's will dictated, his money was used to found Gresham College after his wife's death in 1596. Originally housed in the Gresham mansion and now located in Barnard's Inn Hall in London, the college provides free public lectures in astronomy, divinity, geometry, law, music, physics, rhetoric, and commerce. Gresham also left a share of his wealth to prisons, hospitals, and almshouses (places that housed and fed the poor). But the greatest memorial to Gresham's achievements remained the Royal Exchange. Since its founding, the building has almost always housed some sort of financial trading. Twice destroyed by fire, it was rebuilt both times on the same site. In the first fire, the Great Fire of London in 1666, all the monuments of English kings and queens that adorned the building were destroyed. Miraculously, the only surviving statue was of the Royal Exchange's founder, Sir Thomas Gresham.

The interior of the original Royal Exchange building, crowded with merchants, in 1644

Adam Smith (1723-1790) pioneered the formal study of economics with his famous book The Wealth of Nations, *which analyzed and promoted free trade and capitalism.*

2

Adam Smith
Father of Economics

"*H*e was the most absent man in Company that I ever saw, Moving his Lips and talking to himself, and Smiling," one friend said of Adam Smith. Quiet, sickly, and so absent-minded that he once wandered 15 miles from home in his nightgown, Smith might have seemed an unlikely person to revolutionize economics. But, his friend continued, "If you awak'd him from his Reverie, and made him attend to the Subject of Conversation, he immediately began a Harangue and never stop'd till he told you all he knew about it, with the utmost Philosophical

Ingenuity." In other words, when Smith applied his mind to a topic, he produced long, detailed philosophical arguments. When he applied his mind to economics, he produced an analysis of the economic system of his time that profoundly influenced government policy and economists to come.

In the mid-1700s, the economy of Great Britain stood on the threshold of a period of massive change known as the Industrial Revolution. Previously, goods had been handmade by craftsmen in small workshops. Wood was the only available fuel, and water and wind were the only power sources for machinery. It was not until the use of coal as a fuel increased and the steam engine was invented that people could build useful machines on a large scale. The new machines produced goods more quickly and efficiently than ever before, particularly in the textile industry. As productivity boomed, people rushed to enter the exciting new industries. Those with enough money and ambition built large factories to house their machines and employed hundreds of workers to run them. Industrialization brought hopes of an advancing economy and prosperity for all, and Adam Smith was the first to explain how the new system functioned and how to encourage its growth.

Adam Smith's father, also named Adam, was a lawyer and civil servant who served for a time as comptroller of customs at Kirkcaldy, on the east coast of Scotland. He had been a widower with an 11-year-old son, Hugh, when he married 26-year-old Margaret Douglas in 1720. Less than three years later, while Margaret was pregnant with their first son, Adam Smith Sr. died. The baby, Adam, was born and baptized on June 5, 1723, in Kirkcaldy. Margaret raised her son alone, aided by tutors and guardians designated in her husband's will.

The relationship between mother and son was a particularly close, loving bond, and it was likely Margaret who encouraged Adam in his scholarly ambitions. Adam was a sickly youth, but he excelled academically. From 1729 to 1737, he attended Kirkcaldy's two-room burgh (town) school, where he studied Latin, mathematics, history, and writing.

At age 14, Adam proceeded to Glasgow University, remaining there for three years. Glasgow was a beautiful, prosperous trading center with a population 10 times that of Kirkcaldy. At the university, Adam studied mathematics, political economy (the study of how public policies affect economic and social welfare), and moral philosophy (the study of moral principles and how they affect human behavior). He was heavily influenced by the university's professor of moral philosophy, Francis Hutcheson. A rebel for his time, Hutcheson was the first Glasgow professor to lecture in English instead of traditional Latin. Although this caused a stir among old-timers, it made him well liked by the students. His lectures struck a chord with Adam Smith, who was such an admirer that he attended them three mornings and five afternoons a week.

Francis Hutcheson (1694-1746) taught that justice and economic growth were based on private property and individual rights. He was one of the most noted professors at Glasgow University (below).

Hutcheson believed that ethics and politics were intertwined, and his teachings helped to form some of Smith's early economic thoughts.

Smith did so well at Glasgow that in 1740 he received the Snell Exhibition, a scholarship for talented students interested in becoming clergymen. The scholarship enabled him to study at Balliol College, part of Oxford University in England. That summer, he made the week-long trip to Oxford on horseback. It was the first time Smith had been out of his native country, and the journey expanded his horizons. He immediately noticed how much more advanced England's agricultural and manufacturing systems were than Scotland's. His experience at Oxford was also strikingly different from the academic setting he had relished at Glasgow. Few professors spent their time teaching, and Smith found the experience intellectually stifling.

Luckily, Balliol College had one of the best libraries at Oxford. This gave Smith an opportunity to direct his own studies, and he spent endless hours reading in the library. He devoured French literature, Greek and Latin classics, and philosophy. One day, the heads of the college found Smith reading the recently published philosophy text *A Treatise of Human Nature*, by fellow Scotsman David Hume, a religious skeptic. They immediately confiscated the controversial book and threw it away. Smith realized that his reading interests were not in line with Oxford tradition, nor were they compatible with a career

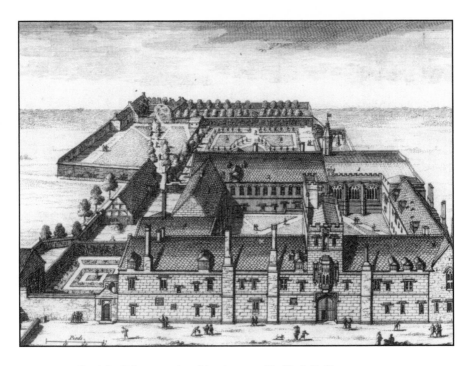

Smith did not enjoy his time at Balliol College because, he believed, there was not enough academic competition or financial incentive to give the Oxford professors a reason to work hard at teaching.

in the church. Adding to his feeling of isolation was the fact that Scots were not popular in England. Smith began to suffer from fits of shaking, probably symptoms of a nervous breakdown. He left Oxford before his scholarship ended, never to return.

In 1746, Smith returned to his mother's home in Scotland without a definite plan. After about a year and a half, however, he was invited to give a series of public lectures in Edinburgh on law, rhetoric, and the history of philosophy. Smith was not a masterful public speaker—listeners described him as having a harsh voice and a stammer—but the lectures were a success. One of the audience members impressed by Smith's scholarship was David Hume. Their meeting began a friendship that lasted nearly 30 years. Throughout that time, Smith and Hume carried on a long correspondence that touched upon both academic topics and personal concerns.

In 1751, Smith's lecturing skills earned him a professorship at Glasgow University to teach logic courses. He also substituted for the professor of moral philosophy, who was ill. When the professor died the following year, Smith took over the chair of moral philosophy, a position he held for 12 years. The job allowed him to teach his favorite subjects—ethics, law, government, theology, and economics. He was a well-respected instructor, and the students enjoyed taking his classes. This was not only heartwarming, but also profitable, since Smith's pay was based on the number of students enrolled in his courses. Smith later said that teaching at Glasgow was "by far the most useful, and, therefore, as by far the happiest and most honorable period of my life."

In 1759, Smith published some of his ethics lectures as *The Theory of Moral Sentiments*. This book, which tried to explain how people make moral decisions, established his scholarly reputation. Hume helped to promote his friend's work by sending copies to influential acquaintances. One of these was Charles Townshend, a member

Adam Smith praised David Hume (1711-1776) as "by far the most illustrious philosopher and historian of the present age." Hume did as much as possible to aid his friend Smith's career.

of Parliament who was highly impressed by the book. Townshend had recently married the countess of Dalkeith and was now searching for a tutor for her 18-year-old son, the third duke of Buccleuch. He decided Smith should tutor his stepson and accompany him on his travels. (In those days, upper-class young men finished off their education with a "Grand Tour" of Europe to develop sophistication.) The appointment was lucrative, with a yearly salary that was double Smith's college earnings, paid traveling expenses while abroad, and a yearly pension after the appointment ended. Moreover, it offered Smith the chance to meet Europe's foremost scholars and to observe different economic and political systems. So, with an offer too good to turn down, Smith resigned from Glasgow in 1764 and joined the young duke on his journey.

Smith spent almost three years as a tutor, traveling mainly around France. He met the famous philosopher Voltaire, whom he greatly admired. He was also able to keep in touch with Hume, who had moved to Paris as secretary to the British embassy. Smith enjoyed the most active phase of his entire social life while in France, attending many plays, operas, and concerts. Although he was described as an unattractive gentleman with bad French and big teeth, he owned an extensive wardrobe of suits and must have made a dashing statement on his evenings out. The fact that his book, *The Theory of Moral Sentiments*, was in vogue in Paris surely helped his allure. The ladies of high society found him particularly charming. There is evidence that Smith may have had at least one romantic attachment, but attention from women mostly embarrassed him and made him nervous.

While in Paris, Smith spent time with François Quesnay, a doctor who was the head of a group of economists called the physiocrats. The group met frequently in Quesnay's apartment, and Smith eagerly joined in their discussions. The physiocrats challenged the prevailing economic theory of mercantilism, which said that nations gained wealth by accumulating gold and silver. Instead, they believed that a country's wealth came from the goods it produced. Although Smith did not agree with their emphasis on agricultural production instead of manufacturing, the discussions further heightened his interest in economics. Especially interesting to him was the physiocrats' concept of *laissez-faire* (French for "allow to do") economics. According to this concept, the market would function best if it were free from the control of mercantilist governments.

Since Smith's tutoring position allowed him a great deal of spare time, he began writing down some of his thoughts on economics. After his job ended in 1766, he returned to Britain and lived mainly in Kirkcaldy and London while developing his ideas into a book. His tutoring pension came in handy, since the two-volume book ended up taking 12 years to complete. *An Inquiry into the Nature and Causes of the Wealth of Nations* was published on March 9, 1776, and rapidly became the most acclaimed economics text to date.

In *The Wealth of Nations*, Smith intended to show how nations produced wealth and how wealth could be increased. He wanted to define the unwritten laws that governed the economic market, the "invisible hand" guiding individuals in society. Smith believed that people produced the goods society wanted due to self-interest. Because they needed to earn a living, they would do the work or sell the things that other people would pay for. Smith wrote, "It is not from the benevolence of the butcher, the brewer, or the baker, that we expect our dinner, but from their regard to their own interest."

The Wealth of Nations *remains so famous that in 1991, a first-edition copy like the one shown here sold at Sotheby's, a London auction house, for 18,500 pounds (about $32,700 at the time).*

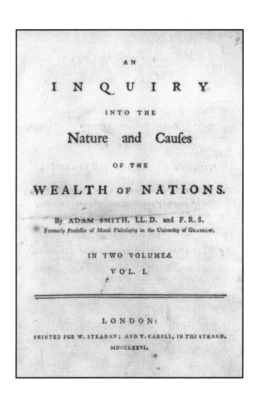

AN

I N Q U I R Y

INTO THE

Nature and Caufes

OF THE

WEALTH OF NATIONS.

By ADAM SMITH, LL. D. and F. R. S.
Formerly Profeffor of Moral Philofophy in the Univerfity of GLASGOW.

IN TWO VOLUMES.

VOL. I.

LONDON:

PRINTED FOR W. STRAHAN; AND T. CADELL, IN THE STRAND.
MDCCLXXVI.

But what prevented self-interested individuals from cheating and exploiting others to benefit themselves? Smith argued that self-interest was checked by free-market competition. Businesspeople may have wanted to charge extremely high prices for goods and services, but they could not get away with it. If they raised the price above a reasonable level, competitors would simply undercut them. People would buy the lower-priced good or service, and the competitors would take away customers. The price that could be charged for a good or service was determined by the market, not by individuals. In the same way, Smith said, the competitive market also decided the prices that employers paid for labor and ensured that businesspeople produced the kinds and quantities of goods and services that consumers wanted. This system became known as capitalism.

Smith concluded that because the market could run itself so well, it was important to encourage it to operate freely and competitively, without government regulation. Although he never used the term, Smith is closely associated with the laissez-faire principle of the physiocrats. He was not anti-government, however. He acknowledged that government was essential to providing national defense, a justice system, and public institutions. Though he opposed excessive taxation, Smith thought that some taxes were necessary to fund government services such as armies, police, roads, and schools.

Smith's main concern was free trade among nations, and he viewed monopolies (business interests so large they can limit competition) and tariffs (government taxes on goods entering a country) as obstacles to the natural workings of the market. At the time, businesspeople organized themselves into guilds, to which the government often granted exclusive rights to deal in certain kinds of merchandise. Similarly, trading companies were granted exclusive rights to trade in certain areas of the world. Smith called these monopolies "a great enemy to good management" because they limited competition, allowing guilds and trading companies to charge unnaturally high prices. He attacked tariffs for the same reason. Designed to protect domestic industries by making imported goods more costly, tariffs also ended up stifling competition. Without the need to compete with foreign products, producers of domestic goods could charge higher prices.

The Wealth of Nations challenged the traditional idea that a nation's wealth came from collecting gold and silver. According to Smith, the wealth of a nation was measured in capital (goods that produce income) and increased only when more goods were produced. The better the machinery, the more goods a country would be able to produce and trade. Smith also noted that the division of labor, or assigning each worker a specialized task, helped

The division of labor in pin manufacturing in 1764, with each worker handling a different part of the process. As Smith described it, "One man draws out the wire, another straights it, a third cuts it, a fourth points it, a fifth grinds it at the top for receiving the head; to make the head requires two or three distinct operations."

significantly increase economic growth. He reported that he had seen pin factories where 10 people, dividing up the tasks between them, produced 48,000 pins a day. Without the division of labor, those individuals could not have made even 20 pins apiece. Such advances in productivity made Smith hugely optimistic about the future of industry. He believed that as business profits increased, the wages of workers would rise and everyone would accumulate more wealth.

The year 1776 brought both joy and sorrow to Smith—the publication of his book, but also the death of David Hume. Hume lived to see *The Wealth of Nations* finished, and upon reading the book he wrote to his friend, "EUGE! BELLE!" (The first word is Greek, meaning "Well done!" and the second is Latin, meaning "Splendid!") Hume died of stomach disease just a few months later, but the book he had praised so highly flourished. The first edition of *The Wealth of Nations* was so popular it sold out within six months. By 1800, it had gone through nine editions and was being read throughout Europe and America. In Smith's lifetime alone, it was translated into Danish, French, German, Italian, and Spanish.

Smith's ideas began to influence politics in Great Britain. In 1777, Prime Minister Lord Frederick North's budget introduced two new taxes based on tax policies advocated in *The Wealth of Nations*. Charles James Fox, the most powerful member of the House of Commons, referred to *The Wealth of Nations* in a 1783 debate in Parliament, causing sales of the book to rise. Prime Minister William Pitt's 1787 Consolidation Bill revised customs regulations according to Smith's free trade models. In 1799, wealthy stockbroker David Ricardo read *The Wealth of Nations* while on vacation and became so enthralled that he decided to become an economist. Twenty years later, Ricardo pushed for free trade as a member of Parliament, notably trying to repeal the 1815 Corn Laws, which placed a tariff on imported grain and had caused grain prices to rise. (The Corn Laws were finally repealed in 1846.)

William Pitt (1759-1806), called "Pitt the Younger" because his father was also a politician, became England's youngest prime minister at the age of 24. Adam Smith's influence led Pitt to make major reforms during his 20 years in office.

Adam Smith (center) walking in Edinburgh, where he spent the later part of his life. This print was made in 1787 by John Kay, an engraver whose shop lay on Smith's daily route to work.

After the publication of *The Wealth of Nations*, Smith served for a time as an adviser to the British government on economic matters. Then, in 1778, he was appointed commissioner of customs in Scotland. He accepted the position and settled in Edinburgh with his mother and other relatives. As customs commissioner, Smith collected taxes on goods from other countries brought into Scotland. Although it seems an ironic job for the most famous advocate of free trade, Smith remained true to his principles by using his position to reform the customs service and reduce excess taxes.

Smith remained a bachelor his entire life. He had nervous, eccentric tendencies (such as talking to himself) and was plagued by spells of imagined illness. But he was a kind man, devoted to friends, relatives, and especially his mother, who died at the old age of 90. Adam Smith lived on six years after his beloved mother's death. He passed away at age 67, on July 17, 1790. On his deathbed, he expressed disappointment that he had not achieved more. He requested that his executors burn the papers he was working on, except those to be published posthumously in *Essays on Philosophical Subjects* (1795).

The years after Adam Smith's death brought many economic changes. In most European countries, democratic movements limited the power of monarchs and guilds, spelling the end of the mercantilist system. The emerging capitalism Smith had described in *The Wealth of Nations* gradually prevailed throughout the world, but not always in a form he would have predicted or approved. Guilds were abolished, but new monopolies arose to take their place. With the advent of large factories during the Industrial Revolution came a new class of business owners, known as capitalists or industrialists, who formed corporations to conduct their business. Some of the largest corporations grew powerful enough to limit competition and raise prices, much as the guilds and trading companies had in Smith's time. Some industrialists manipulated Smith's ideas to justify their practices. They opposed attempts to protect workers from inhumane working conditions or to limit the power of monopolies, arguing that such interference would restrict the free market. In the United States, monopolies were outlawed in 1890 by the Sherman Antitrust Act, but they remain an important issue today, as does the balance between government regulation and free operation of the market.

Smith's theories have sometimes been misinterpreted, but they endure. Since most economies in the twenty-first century have adopted some level of capitalism, his ideas may seem obvious today. But during his time, they were visionary. He provided the framework of concepts—supply and demand, self-interest, competition, and free markets—used by nearly every economist who came after him. As the nineteenth-century German economist Friedrich von Hermann remarked, "Whoever understands something of economics has to regard himself, with respect to the chief principles of this science, as a disciple of Adam Smith."

Although times have changed since he wrote *The Wealth of Nations*, Smith's philosophy can still be applied to modern life. The Adam Smith Institute in London, for example, is an enduring tribute to Smith's work. Through policy reports and seminars, the institute examines ways in which people can have more freedom to make economic decisions. Dr. Madsen Pirie, director of the institute, says that one of the major lessons people can learn from Adam Smith is "a basic respect for others. Instead of trying to impose his own plans on his fellow men and women, Smith recognized their right to live by their own values, and value their own priorities. Although some people claim that ordinary people are not clever enough to plan their own lives, Smith saw that they usually made a far better job of it than governments or bureaucrats manage to do."

Thomas Robert Malthus (1766-1834) roused controversy with his theory that the world's population, unless controlled, would outgrow the resources needed to support it.

3

Thomas Robert Malthus
The Population Prophet

*H*e was the "best-abused man of the age." His critics called him an atheist, a pessimist, a plagiarist, a hypocrite, and "a shameless sycophant of the ruling classes." He was accused of defending smallpox, slavery, and the murder of children. Yet he was an honest, gentle scholar and clergyman. Those who knew him said that he "could hate nobody" and "no one could know him without loving him." Even one of his opponents acknowledged that he had "made as unquestionable an addition to the theory of political economy as any writer for a century past." How could a pleasant young man like Thomas Robert Malthus inspire so much outrage?

Malthus's ideas were misinterpreted throughout his lifetime, and he remains probably the most misunderstood economist to date. His intentions were noble: to find and explain the causes of poverty and social misery so that they could be prevented. He produced theories that influenced future economists and are still relevant today. But throughout his career he faced controversy and strong opposition, because his kindness was hidden behind a bleak message.

Thomas Robert Malthus was born on February 13, 1766, in the town of Wooton in Surrey, England. Robert, as he was called, was the sixth of seven children born into Daniel and Henrietta Malthus's upper-middle-class home. Daniel, an eccentric country gentleman, had inherited enough money to support his family without working. He was a cultured man, a friend of philosophers David Hume and Jean Jacques Rousseau. He spent his time on scholarly pursuits, such as science—especially botany— and foreign literature. Daniel strongly influenced Robert's personal and intellectual development. Although the two did not agree on every issue, they shared many common interests, including a love of London theater and country life. Robert had a close relationship with his family and friends throughout his lifetime. He was known to be a quiet, affectionate, and cheerful young man, routinely described as handsome.

The Malthus home in Wooton, Surrey, known as "the Rookery"

Robert was instructed by his father until he was 10 years old, and then by his father's handpicked private tutors. In 1784, at the age of 18, he enrolled in Jesus College at Cambridge University. He quickly became recognized as an exceptional scholar, earning awards in Greek, Latin, and English oratory. He graduated in 1788 with an honors degree in mathematics. In the same year, he was ordained as a clergyman, despite some concern voiced by the Master of Jesus College that his speech impediment (a result of being born with a cleft palate) might hold him back in the church. Robert became a curate at Okewood Chapel in Albury, near his family's home in Surrey. He enjoyed a serene country life, performing his pastoral duties for the village chapel.

In 1793, Robert was elected a fellow of Jesus College. Being a fellow was a prestigious appointment, given only to those who graduated with high honors. The fellowship allowed him to participate in governing the school and provided him with a salary from the college revenue.

Okewood Chapel, where Robert Malthus was a clergyman

The First Court of Jesus College as it looked in the nineteenth century

During his fellowship, he lived only occasionally at the college, but it was there that he began to formulate his economic thoughts. His first attempt was in 1796 with the pamphlet *The Crisis, a View of the Present Interesting State of Great Britain, by a Friend to the Constitution.* Sadly, no copy of the manuscript—which protested the administration of Prime Minister William Pitt—has survived. Although Robert was unable to find a publisher for the work, the writing proved he was willing to take a stand on controversial topics.

61

Robert returned home often to visit his father. Like many leisured gentlemen of the day, Daniel Malthus enjoyed a stimulating intellectual debate, and Robert was always up for the challenge. One discussion between them centered on the popular question of whether the human condition could be improved. In the late 1700s, the Industrial Revolution was transforming Great Britain. High-powered factory machines dramatically increased the output of goods, which raised the standard of living

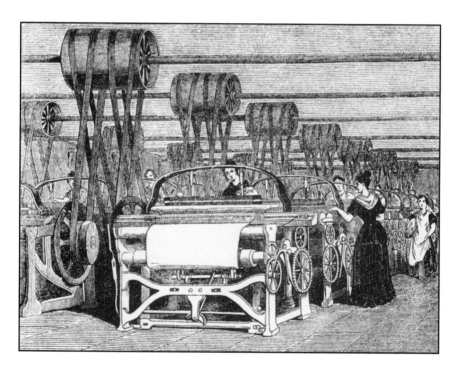

The English textile industry led the way in the Industrial Revolution with advances such as the power loom, invented around 1785 to weave cloth automatically.

for many people. For much of the working class, however, industrialization also brought upheaval and struggle. Former agricultural laborers now toiled long hours in huge factories and lived in crowded, filthy city slums. Philosophers and champions of social justice theorized about ways to improve the lives of the working people. But in spite of the widespread poverty, there was a mood of optimism in the evolving economy. Many thinkers believed that the social and economic progress then underway would eventually transform society into a utopia, or perfect state.

Utopian thinkers, including Daniel Malthus, argued that an increasing population meant more total happiness. With more people working, society would produce more goods, which would increase the standard of living for everyone. Rapid growth was a sign of a nation's strength. Many believed, however, that the English population had not grown fast enough in the past century, or even that it had decreased. There was no real way to be sure, since reliable census figures did not exist at the time. But Robert was convinced that England's population was swelling. Furthermore, he thought that with the increasing number of mouths to feed, reaching a state of utopia was doubtful. In an effort to convince his father, he began writing his thoughts down. The result, in 1798, was an anonymously published book called *An Essay on the Principle of Population as it Affects the Future Improvement of Society.*

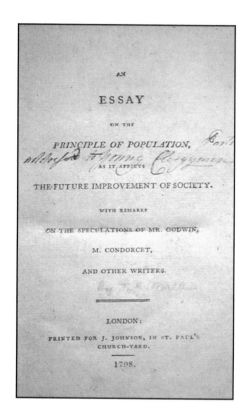

A first-edition copy of An Essay on the Principle of Population *from Malthus's own collection. Malthus claimed he wrote the book "with an intention of merely stating his thoughts to his friend upon paper in a clearer manner than he thought he could do in conversation."*

Not many copies of the book circulated, but it still caused quite a stir. Robert Malthus's basic theory stated that population naturally tended to increase faster than the supply of food. He started with two premises: that people would always need to eat and that they would continue to reproduce. But, he said, the ability of population to increase was much greater than the ability of the earth to provide food for that population. Malthus claimed that population grew by a geometric ratio (in which one number keeps multiplying itself by another). In fact, he calculated that the population would tend to double every

25 years—a shocking idea, considering seventeenth-century statisticians had predicted that it would take 600 years for the population to double. But the food supply, Malthus said, increased only by an arithmetic ratio (in which one number is repeatedly added to another). The result, he stated, was that "the human species would increase as the numbers 1, 2, 4, 8, 16, 32, 64, 128, 256, and the subsistence as 1, 2, 3, 4, 5, 6, 7, 8, 9. In two centuries the population would be to the means of subsistence as 256 to 9; in three centuries as 4,096 to 13, and in two thousand years the difference would be almost incalculable." If population growth could be stunted, the food supply could temporarily catch up to the population. But then the increased prosperity would encourage more people to reproduce, and the population would build up again. The food supply could never increase fast enough so that everyone would eat better, only so that more people could eat the same small amount of food. Instead of advancing toward utopia, Malthus concluded, "human life has a melancholy hue."

Malthus's population theory brought a whole spectrum of responses—fear, misinterpretation, disagreement, and praise. The interest and debate over his ideas prompted him to do more research on the subject of population. He traveled to Scandinavia and Russia in 1799 and France and Switzerland in 1802, gathering historical information, social observations, and demographic records. In 1801, England published its first official census, which showed that the population had increased dramatically in the past century. Malthus incorporated all this research into a second edition of his book, which, at roughly 200,000 words, contained more theory and data than the 55,000-word first edition. The title was changed to *An Essay on the Principle of Population, or a View of its Past and Present Effects on Human Happiness, with an Inquiry into our Prospects Respecting the Future Removal or Mitigation of the Evils which it Occasions.* As the new name suggests, the second edition was slightly less severe in tone. Instead of emphasizing the biological laws that governed population growth, Malthus shifted his concentration to the social effects of overpopulation and how population could be limited. But the essential message of doom remained unchanged in all six editions that were published during his lifetime.

Malthus wrote that the burgeoning population had historically been checked by war, famine, and disease, which raise the death rate. Population growth could also be slowed through preventative checks—lowering the birth rate. In his second edition, Malthus offered hope that "moral restraint" might be used as a preventative check. In other words, he wanted people to avoid reproducing outside of marriage and to marry at an older age, thus decreasing the number of children they had. He also believed that people should not have any more children than they could support. (Malthus did not, however, advocate contraception, rejecting the idea on religious grounds.) Since the middle and upper classes already had fewer children, Malthus's main aim was lowering the birth rate of the working class.

Malthus's theories tied in directly to the controversial issue of the English Poor Laws. Essentially a welfare system set up around 1600, the Poor Laws established a public responsibility for care of the poor. The laws worked efficiently at first, but by the end of the 1700s, rising food prices and the social changes brought by industrialization made the system increasingly costly to

A poor woman and her starving child trudge through the snow in this 1839 book illustration. A factory looms in the background, a reminder that many people in the nineteenth century blamed the plight of the poor on industrialization.

carry out. Reforming the laws became a matter of intense public debate. In *An Essay*, Malthus called for the gradual abolition of the Poor Laws. He believed that assistance for the poor increased the population while decreasing the food supply. Making the poor comfortable only encouraged them to have more children. Furthermore, charity took food and wages from working people and gave them to the poor, who did not work to produce anything themselves. Malthus believed that poor people would be better off being independent, having higher-wage jobs, and practicing moral restraint than being dependent on low-wage public service employment and having large, hungry families. He wrote, "I feel persuaded that if the Poor Laws had never existed in this country, though there might have been a few instances of very severe distress, the aggregate mass of happiness among the common people would have been much greater than it is at present."

Malthus's argument was persuasive. As early as 1800, Prime Minister William Pitt—who had supported an increase in relief for large families four years earlier— changed his opinion after reading the first edition of *An Essay* and withdrew his support for a new bill for poor relief. In 1834, citing Malthus as an influence, politicians reformed the Poor Laws completely. Assistance for the poor was reduced to an extremely low level, below the standard of living of the poorest worker, to discourage the poor from multiplying or becoming dependent. Malthus and his supporters always claimed that their purpose was

*The reform of the Poor Laws did little to curtail the
need for relief programs such as this London soup
kitchen, where the poor lined up for food in 1844.*

to improve the lives of the poor, but their views were
widely criticized as inhumane, and the reforms proved to
have little impact on poverty.

Although Malthus's population theory defined him
as a scholar and permeated many of his writings, he produced a wide variety of pamphlets and articles after the
second edition of *An Essay*. He continued his religious
work, as well. In 1803, he was appointed to another
parish, Walesby, in Lincolnshire. This time he was
retained as rector of the pastorate and was able to draw an

income until his death. He officiated there only occasionally; as was common practice at the time, he employed a curate to hold services in his place. In 1804, Malthus married his cousin, Harriet Eckersall. (Interestingly, she was 27 when they married, an age Malthus suggested for marriage in *An Essay*. He was 38.) The position as rector provided him with the financial security to support a family, although Jesus College policy forced him to give up his fellowship upon marriage. Eventually, three children—Henry, Emily, and Lucy—were born to the Malthuses' happy union.

In 1805, Malthus was appointed "Professor of General History, Politics, Commerce, and Finance" at the newly founded East India College in Hertfordshire. The position was essentially the first professorship in economics in Britain. The institution trained employees of the East India Company for civil service positions in India. The students—who on admission ranged in age from 15 to 22—were instructed in Indian languages, classical languages, mathematics, history, and the English legal system. Malthus proudly held the job until his death, fondly called "Pop" by his students.

Beginning in 1809, Malthus became intrigued by a series of letters written to the *Morning Chronicle* newspaper by economist David Ricardo, addressing the price of gold. Malthus disagreed with Ricardo on some points, and the two debated each other in published essays on currency and trade issues. At last, Malthus wrote to

Ricardo that since "we are mainly on the same side of the question, we might supersede the necessity of a long controversy in print . . . by an amicable discussion in private." Apparently, Ricardo had been about to make the same suggestion, and the two met in 1811, beginning a lifelong friendship. Malthus and Ricardo exchanged frequent letters on social and economic dilemmas of the time, each using the other as a sounding board for his thoughts. Ricardo agreed with Malthus's concern over the rising population and its effect on poverty. He feared that the increasing population would lead to a shortage of fertile land. There was only so much fertile ground, and

David Ricardo (1772-1823) made a fortune as a stockbroker by the age of 25 and later became a member of Parliament. As an economist, he is best known for his "iron law of wages," which states that workers' pay rates tend to stabilize at subsistence level.

as the population grew, more people would need to be fed. More labor would be necessary to produce food from the less fertile land, which would have the effect of decreasing wages. Ricardo and Malthus differed on many other issues, but they enjoyed their thoughtful arguments. Before Ricardo's death in 1823, he wrote to Malthus, "I should not like you more than I do if you agreed in opinion with me." Malthus later said of his friend, "I never loved anybody out of my own family so much."

In 1820, Malthus published his other major economic work, *Principles of Political Economy*. The book commented on the arguments made by Adam Smith in *The Wealth of Nations*. Like many of his contemporaries, Malthus was an ardent student of Smith; he disagreed with him, however, on one important point. Economists like Smith and Ricardo believed that if there were goods available, consumers would always buy them—people had an infinite desire for more goods and would spend money if they had it. Therefore, supply created its own demand.

Malthus, however, argued that economies could suffer "gluts," or temporary dips in business activity (also called recessions), because sometimes manufacturers supplied more goods than people wanted to buy. Consumers might have the money to buy all the goods that were available, but they might prefer to save or hoard their money. Ricardo countered that the money people saved in banks was still being spent because it was lent out to others, but Malthus maintained his belief that low demand caused gluts. Although Ricardo's ideas prevailed at the time, the economist John Maynard Keynes would refer to Malthus's work in the 1930s to explain why he thought the economy could not recover from the Great Depression without government intervention.

Despite his controversial theories, Malthus was honored throughout his lifetime. In 1819, he was elected a member of the Royal Society, a group dedicated to promoting excellence in science. Along with Ricardo, he was one of the 20 original members of the Political Economy Club, founded in London in 1821. In 1824, he was elected one of the 10 royal associates of the Royal Academy of Literature. Malthus was also one of the founders of the Statistical Society of London in 1834, and he received several awards in France and Germany.

Malthus's principle of population was adopted by a variety of other thinkers. He influenced Charles Darwin,

Naturalist Charles Darwin (1809-1882) incorporated Malthus's ideas about population into his theory of evolution.

who read *An Essay* in October 1838 and decided to apply Malthus's argument to plants and animals. Darwin argued that because populations increase faster than the supply of food, living creatures must compete for survival. Populations are checked through famine and disease, and only creatures best adapted to their environments survive to produce the next generation and to pass on their traits. Malthus's ideas were also applied to the birth-control movement. Although he opposed contraception, his name was routinely attached to organizations like the Malthusian League, founded in 1877 to promote new birth-control methods. And a century later, concerns over the "population explosion" and energy crises aroused a new interest in Malthus. People worried that the expanding population would deplete the world's supply of nonrenewable resources, such as oil.

Was Malthus right? Did he have a premonition about population? Today, the world has a record population of more than 6 billion. This number continues to grow by 77 million a year and could increase to 9 billion by the year 2050. And while the majority of people have enough to eat, many do not. According to the United Nations, about 841 million people are chronically malnourished—nearly one-sixth of the world. A connection definitely exists between population and poverty, and there is little debate that Malthus should be credited for bringing attention to the issue. He did not, however, have his mathematical relationship right. Population has greatly increased—but due to advances in agricultural technology, our ability to feed ourselves has kept up. In 1700, production of food was no higher than it had been 2,000 years before. But from 1700 to 1800, the innovations of the Industrial Revolution doubled England's agricultural output. Today, output is so high that only 3 percent of the world's population works in agriculture, yet they produce enough to feed everyone (although it is not distributed equally). While Malthus's critics see this as proof against his theories, his supporters continue to warn that the population may still someday outgrow the earth's resources.

Accuracy aside, Malthus had a lasting influence on economics. After reading *An Essay*, the nineteenth-century writer Thomas Carlyle called economics the "dismal science"—a term that is still used by many, although somewhat humorously, to describe the field today. The famous communist Karl Marx was a staunch critic, believing Malthus did not care for the working people and had aligned himself with the ruling class. But the list of admirers is also long. British economist John Stuart Mill, for instance, said Malthus's population theory was the beginning of all reasonable thinking on the subject of wages and poverty.

Malthus died on December 29, 1834, of a heart attack. The man who was so concerned about population growth left no living descendants. Of his three children, Henry and Emily both married, but neither had children; Lucy died near adulthood.

Described as "domineering, impetuous, passionate, full of boundless self-confidence," Karl Marx (1818-1883) was one of the most famous revolutionary thinkers in history. His economic theories supported his belief that capitalism would be replaced by communism.

4

Karl Marx
The Revolutionary Economist

The era of economic progress called the Industrial Revolution brought enormous wealth for a select few: the owners of the new mass-producing factories. But for the workers—men, women, and children as young as five—who slaved in these hot, dirty, and unsafe factories, often for 18-hour days, progress was less easy to see. Many were paid so little that they had trouble affording food, clothing, and shelter. Economists largely supported the rising class of factory owners, arguing that some poverty was natural in a competitive free-market economy. A number of people in the early nineteenth century, however, were looking for a better way to organize society so that all of its members would benefit. Some, especially in European countries ruled by monarchs with absolute power, saw democracy as a solution, and they struggled for freedom of speech and more participation in government. Others organized workers to campaign for better working conditions and higher pay. More radical thinkers, however, believed that the capitalist economy could not be reformed; instead, it should be completely overthrown—by revolution if necessary. They supported communism, a system in which property would belong to all citizens in common and differences in social class would no longer exist.

The most famous of these thinkers was Karl Marx, a German philosopher who launched—and lent his name to—an international communist movement. Marxism later became associated with subversive politics, violent revolution, and repressive dictatorships. But Marx himself achieved little politically and did not write much about actual communism. His achievement was as an economist who provided an economic basis for the communist movement. Convinced that capitalism was destined to fail, Marx set out to prove his theory by producing a massive analysis of the system and its flaws. The result was a vivid portrait of class struggle, a call for an entirely new economic system, and a critique of the study of economics and all economists who had come before.

Karl Marx was born in the city of Trier, Prussia (a powerful German state), on May 5, 1818, into a comfortable middle-class family. He was the second son of Heinrich and Henrietta Marx, who ultimately had four sons and five daughters. His Dutch mother was an uneducated woman who never learned to read or speak German fluently. His father was an accomplished Jewish lawyer who later became a justice of the peace. Because Jews in Trier were banned from professional practice and public office, Heinrich had adopted Christianity for himself and his family. Karl grew up happily, an intelligent, robust boy who loved telling stories and playing pranks.

Trier as it looked when Karl Marx was a child. One of the oldest cities in Germany, Trier was founded by the Romans in about 15 B.C.

After completing his early schooling in Trier, Karl entered Bonn University at the age of 17 to study law, as his father had hoped. But he devoted little energy to his studies. Instead, he spent a great deal of time socializing and accumulating large debts, which his disappointed father paid off. During his first year, Karl was imprisoned for drunkenness, caught with a "prohibited weapon" (a pistol), and even involved in a duel. In 1836, Heinrich allowed his rowdy son to transfer to the more academic University of Berlin in the hope that he would settle down. The move was a good one for Karl. Although he still ran up debts and rarely attended classes, he devoted much of the next four years to reading and writing on his own. His studies, however, had turned towards philosophy, a subject his father thought impractical. He became increasingly estranged from his family, and when Heinrich died in 1838, Karl did not attend the funeral.

In Berlin, Karl became a fan of the writings of Friedrich Hegel, who had been a professor of philosophy at the university from 1818 until his death in 1831. In Hegel's philosophy, human history was shaped by ideas. Out of the dialectic (conflict) between opposing ideas, new ideas would be formed, and society would evolve toward perfection. Hegel, a conservative, believed that Prussia was ideal because it was governed by absolute monarchy, which he thought the highest form of government. Karl Marx, however, joined a radical group called the Young Hegelians that applied a left-wing interpretation

Georg Wilhelm Friedrich Hegel (1770-1831) incorporated his interest in ethics, aesthetics, history, and religion into his philosophy.

to Hegel's philosophy, questioning government and religion and discussing the theory of communism. Marx was interested in Hegel's idea that the world was constantly changing as a result of struggles between opposing forces. But he rejected Hegel's idealism, concentrating instead on the material world of basic human needs.

When Frederick William VI became king of Prussia in 1840, he appointed many conservatives to government and education positions. His regime censored publications and persecuted anyone who disagreed with it. Since Marx's dissertation essay was philosophically radical, he thought it was unlikely that the conservative professors at Berlin would grant him a degree. He sent his manuscript to the University of Jena, a small institution quick to grant diplomas, and in 1841 he was awarded his doctorate.

Marx now needed to earn his own living. He wanted to teach philosophy, but he knew he could not secure a job at a university because of his radical leanings. He turned to journalism, and in May 1842 he began working for the *Rheinische Zeitung*, a small liberal democratic newspaper in Cologne. By October, Marx's talent for writing had won him an appointment as editor in chief. He wrote editorials on a variety of issues, including freedom of the press. After repeatedly attacking government censorship restrictions, Marx received numerous warnings from the Prussian authorities to alter the tone of the paper, but he refused to oblige. The last straw came when he wrote negatively about the tsar of Russia, an important ally of Prussia. The Prussian government closed the newspaper. Seeing that a battle for liberalism was impossible in Prussia, Marx decided to move to Paris. He quickly married his beautiful childhood friend, Jenny von Westphalen, and the two set forth for France in September 1843.

In Paris, Marx edited and wrote for several short-lived radical German newspapers. His radicalism had been mainly philosophical in the past, but now his interest turned toward politics and economics, especially the unwillingness of the wealthy ruling elite to help improve the condition of the working classes. Increasingly convinced that economics were at the root of all social and political issues, Marx began studying writings by classical economists such as Adam Smith, David Ricardo, and John Stuart Mill. He also made contact with workers' associations and became more sympathetic to communism. He outlined his new ideas in an 1844 series of writings, *Economic and Philosophical Manuscripts* (which was not published until 1932). In it, Marx criticized the existing social order, suggesting that the capitalist system alienated and dehumanized workers. Like many of his friends, he saw communism as a solution, supporting a major upheaval of society—even revolution—to abolish private property and make all citizens equal.

It was in Paris in 1844 that Marx met 23-year-old Friedrich Engels, the radical son of a wealthy German textile manufacturer. Engels had just finished writing a book about poor working conditions in the industrial towns of northern England, *The Condition of the Working Class in England in 1844.* The two men found they shared virtually identical views on the problems of capitalism, and so began their lifelong friendship and collaboration. But the friends would not stay long in Paris. Marx had published anti-Prussian articles in a newspaper, and the Prussian government was angry. In 1845, at the request of the Prussian authorities, Marx was expelled from France.

Marx moved to Belgium, and Engels soon joined him. Both became involved in the Communist League, an international association of workers formed in 1847. The group assigned the task of preparing a statement of

From his experience with his father's business, Friedrich Engels (1820-1895) had a firsthand understanding of capitalism that proved valuable to Marx's work. Even more importantly, Engels was one of the few people able to read Marx's scrawling handwriting.

its principles to Marx and Engels. In six weeks, Marx penned a 23-page pamphlet from some notes Engels had written, adding detailed analysis to Engels's basic ideas. The draft the two submitted, published in early 1848, was the now-famous *Communist Manifesto*, the first comprehensive statement of modern communism.

Marx and Engels's theory said that every social order was based on the production and exchange of goods. Throughout history, each system of producing and exchanging goods had divided people into ruled and ruling classes. The ruling class created laws, government, religion, and philosophy that supported the economic system. But the economic system was always evolving.

New inventions and ideas changed the process of production and the relationship between classes. When the old ruling class resisted the change, trying to hold on to the former economic system and the laws and government that supported it, class conflict developed. Gradually, however, the new system triumphed and a new ruling class was born. History was a chronicle of these struggles between social classes.

Marx and Engels believed one of these struggles was occurring in their time. The Industrial Revolution had changed the process of production into a factory system and created a new ruling class of factory owners. Marx and Engels argued that factories turned the production of goods into an organized, centralized, communal process, but the laws and government still supported the individualistic idea of private property. This conflict between the economic system and the social system, they predicted, would end in a worldwide revolution in which the ruling class would be overthrown by the oppressed proletarians, or working people. Capitalism would self-destruct and be replaced by a communist system in which all members of society planned production and shared property. Since there would be no social classes, there would be no class struggle; having reached its most perfect form, the economy would no longer evolve.

Marx and Engels did not dwell on the practical details of how a communist society would work, but their warnings about the downfall of capitalism were forceful.

"The Communists disdain to conceal their views and aims," concluded the manifesto. "They openly declare that their ends can be attained only by the forcible overthrow of all existing social conditions. Let the ruling classes tremble at a Communist revolution. The proletarians have nothing to lose but their chains. They have a world to win. WORKING MEN OF ALL COUNTRIES, UNITE!"

Scarcely had copies of the *Communist Manifesto* been distributed than the violent revolutions of 1848 erupted in Europe. Working people rioted throughout major cities in France, Belgium, Italy, Germany, and Austria, demanding basic rights such as trial by jury, freedom of speech,

"A spectre is haunting Europe—the spectre of Communism," warned the opening lines of The Communist Manifesto.

and right to assembly. The revolts were unorganized, but intense and violent. Despite some temporary victories, they eventually failed almost everywhere, leaving government policies largely unchanged.

The revolutions had not been organized by communists or inspired by the *Communist Manifesto*, but the Belgian government still wanted radicals like Karl Marx out of the country. Exiled, Marx moved first to Paris and then back to Cologne, where he founded a newspaper, the *Neue Rheinische Zeitung*, to campaign for liberal democracy. He was eventually expelled from Prussia and turned again to France, only to be exiled there, too. At last, in 1849, he settled permanently in London, where he would spend the rest of his life working to support the basic doctrines outlined in the *Communist Manifesto*.

Marx became a political correspondent for the *New York Daily Tribune*, and the large, influential newspaper published several hundred articles by him (some ghostwritten by Engels) over the next decade. Even with this income, Marx was barely able to support his family. He ran up huge debts trying to maintain a middle-class standard of living, which included spacious homes, servants, and private schooling for his children. Often, the family lived in near-poverty and starvation, surviving on the financial support they received from Engels, who worked for his father's company in northern England. Many of Marx's letters to Engels requested urgent help to pay for medicine, groceries, and rent.

Though Marx could sometimes be selfish and demanding, Engels faithfully embezzled small amounts of money from his family's business to send to his friend along with part of his own salary. Similarly, although Jenny Marx lived a destitute and itinerant existence with her husband, the Marxes remained a devoted couple. They had six children, though only three lived into adulthood: Jenny, born in 1844; Laura, in 1846; and Eleanor, in 1855. Eleanor accompanied her father to communist meetings and became involved in working-class politics, while Jenny and Laura both married French communists.

Marx and Engels stand behind Marx's daughters, (from left to right) Jenny, Eleanor, and Laura, in 1864.

Marx remained involved in trying to build an international workers' movement. The Communist League dissolved in 1852 after the Prussian police imprisoned members of the board, so Marx worked with other radicals to form another organization. In 1864, the International Working Men's Association was established in London with Marx as one of its leaders. The International was a group of independent workers' organizations from different countries, whose goal was to unite all workers to achieve political power. The group became best known for its participation in the Paris Commune of 1871, a bloody uprising of defiant Paris citizens against the French government that was ultimately defeated. Although its part in the uprising had been slight, the International gained a reputation as a vast, dangerous conspiracy, and its major members—especially Marx—became infamous. In reality, though, the group did little politically, was plagued by internal power struggles, and dissolved in 1876.

Marx passed most of his time reading books and newspapers at the British Museum or working at home, where, a Prussian police spy reported, "he leads the existence of a real bohemian intellectual. Washing, grooming, and changing his linen are things he does rarely, and he likes to get drunk. Though he is often idle for days on end, he will work day and night with tireless endurance when he has a great deal of work to do. He has no fixed times for going to sleep and waking up. He often stays up all night, and then lies down fully clothed

Friedrich Engels's 1865 membership card for the International Working Men's Association. The fifth signature is Marx's.

on the sofa at midday and sleeps till evening." The result of these eccentric work habits was Marx's masterpiece—*Capital*, an extensive historical examination of capitalism. The first volume, published in 1867, took him 18 years to write. He continued work on the manuscript for the remainder of his life, and three additional volumes were published after his death.

In *Capital*, Marx analyzed the economic laws governing capitalism in an effort to show how the system would eventually collapse. Following the theories of classical economists such as David Ricardo, Marx said that the "value" of a commodity was based on the amount of labor put into making it. If it took twice as much work to make a table than a hat, the table would sell for twice the price of the hat. Supposedly, a worker's labor was also worth as much as the products he or she made. But if workers were paid for the value of the goods they made and the goods sold for the same value, factory owners, or capitalists, would never earn money. To make a profit (which Marx called surplus value), the capitalists paid workers a subsistence wage—only enough to survive and continue working, far less than the value they contributed to the business. And if the capitalists wanted to make a larger profit, they squeezed more labor out of their workers by making them work longer hours for the same pay. If they wanted to work at all, the workers had to endure the unsafe conditions, long workdays, and paltry wages dictated by the capitalists, who controlled the equipment necessary to make the goods.

Marx argued that the competitive capitalist system forced factory owners to exploit their workers to stay in business. If they did not make enough profit to expand their business, they would be beaten by their competitors. Expanding a business, however, meant hiring more workers, which meant spending more money on wages. To solve this problem, capitalists bought machines to replace workers. But it is impossible to get surplus value from a machine, which—unlike a human worker—is purchased for the amount it is worth. Eventually, profits would start

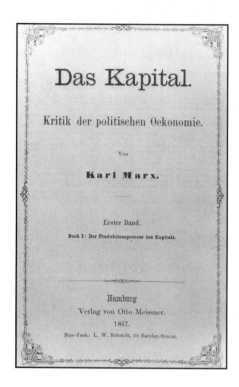

Das Kapital.

Kritik der politischen Oekonomie.

Von

Karl Marx.

Erster Band.

Buch I: Der Produktionsprocess des Kapitals.

Hamburg
Verlag von Otto Meissner.
1867.
New-York: L. W. Schmidt, 24 Barclay-Street.

"I don't suppose anyone has written about 'money' when so short of the stuff," Marx *quipped while writing* Capital. *(Because he wrote it in his native language, the book is often known by its German title,* Das Kapital.*)*

to drop. Without the machines, however, companies could not keep up with their competitors.

The capitalists were in a no-win situation. Profits would continue to decline, and—due to the rising number of unemployed workers—consumers would buy less goods. The result would be an economic recession. Marx agreed with the classical economists that such crises would eventually resolve themselves, but he believed that each would be longer and more severe than the one before. Capitalism was fundamentally unstable, and it would ultimately break down. Competition would eliminate small businesses, leaving only a few companies with all the power and wealth. Meanwhile, the workers would become more numerous, miserable, and rebellious, until at last they overthrew the system. As Marx wrote, "along with the constantly diminishing number of the magnates of capital . . . grows the mass of misery, oppression, slavery, degradation, exploitation; but with this too grows the revolt of the working class, a class always increasing in numbers, and disciplined, united, organized by the very mechanism of the process of capitalist production itself."

The later volumes of *Capital* remained unfinished due to the poor health that plagued Marx's later years, hampering his writing and political work. Marx was grief-stricken when his wife, Jenny, died of cancer in December 1881. Another blow struck when his eldest daughter, Jenny, also succumbed to the disease in January 1883. Karl Marx died two months later, after a long battle with pleurisy (inflammation of the lungs), on March 14, 1883.

Marx's forceful personality had won him few personal friends; only eight people attended his funeral. Engels gave a speech, which began, "On the 14th of March, at a quarter to three in the afternoon, the greatest living thinker ceased to think. He had been left alone for scarcely two minutes, and when we came back we found him in his armchair, peacefully gone to sleep—but for ever." Marx was buried in Highgate Cemetery in London. Engels lived until 1895, dedicating the rest of his life to editing Marx's unfinished manuscript of *Capital*. As his final tribute, Engels willed all his property to Marx's daughters.

Marx's influence was not monumental during his lifetime, but after his death Marxism grew into a worldwide force. His ideas were utilized by many political groups and were even used to form new governments. Most notably, Vladimir Lenin interpreted Marxist theories to create a communist society in Russia after the 1917 revolution. The Russian Revolution, however, was not a culmination of Marx's predictions. Capitalism had not failed in Russia; it had never fully existed there. The economy had still been based on feudalism, in which peasants performed agricultural labor for wealthy landowners, and the revolution was mainly inspired by massive hunger and other problems caused by World War I. The government quickly became a dictatorship and brought little economic advancement for the people, though communism persisted in Russia until the early 1990s. Other countries established communist governments in the twentieth century, but most eventually failed. Although communism still has its supporters, it is clear that the collapse of capitalism Marx predicted has not come true.

Capitalism proved far more versatile than the rigid, self-destructive machine Marx described. Some of the problems he saw in the system—such as a vast disparity between rich and poor—still exist, but new technology and increasing economic development have raised the standard of living for nearly everyone, including the working class. The political climate has changed as well. In Marx's time, nations were controlled by wealthy ruling

Striking French workers in 1995 carry a large picture of Karl Marx, demonstrating that his influence lives on more than 100 years after his death.

classes and monarchs with absolute power. These groups had little interest in fixing the flaws of a system that benefitted them, even if vast numbers of their people were living in poverty. But the rise of democracy created a new philosophy of government that addressed the concerns of average citizens. Most major governments now sponsor social welfare programs that provide public education, health care, and unemployment relief in an effort to give people of all classes the opportunity to survive and prosper. Whether any of these changes are a result of Marx's warnings of crisis and revolution is difficult to say. But part of his legacy, along with the growth of international communism, is the idea that capitalism can undergo serious scrutiny and adaptation.

By supporting a major role for government spending in the economy, John Maynard Keynes (1883-1946) hoped to create "a system where we can act as an organized community for common purposes and to promote economic and social justice."

5

John Maynard Keynes
Shaping the World Economy

The Great Depression of the 1930s was the longest, most severe business slump the United States had ever seen. At its worst, 16 million people, one-third of the workforce, were unemployed, and business production was cut in half. The stock market plummeted, factories stood idle, banks collapsed, and thousands of businesses failed. The international economy was severely shaken. Throughout the crisis, most economists maintained that the market would eventually correct itself. As the Depression dragged on, however, people began to demand active measures to end the devastation. And British economist John Maynard Keynes had a clear solution: pump money into the economy through increased government spending. It was useless to wait for the economy to smooth itself out in the long run; after all, Keynes wrote, "In the long run we are all dead." His revolutionary theories changed the course of government policy around the world and launched an entirely new school of economics.

John Maynard Keynes (pronounced CANES)—usually known as Maynard—was born into a high-achieving family in Cambridge, England, on June 5, 1883. His father, John Neville Keynes, an acclaimed economist and author, was a lecturer in moral sciences at Cambridge University. His mother, Florence Brown Keynes, one of the first women to attend the university, was active in local government and served for a time as the first female mayor of the city of Cambridge. Maynard's younger sister, Margaret, would later be a social worker, and his younger brother, Geoffrey, became a doctor. The Keyneses lived the life of a comfortable, academic Victorian family, enjoying books, theater, and concerts.

As a child, Maynard was sickly and uncoordinated, and he was convinced he was unattractive. Others, however, found him bright, charming, and eager to please. After attending local schools, he won a scholarship to the prestigious school of Eton in 1897. He was an outstanding student, winning dozens of academic prizes during his five years there. Maynard was also elected to an exclusive

*Maynard
Keynes as an
Eton student,
at age 13*

Eton social club known as Pop, and he became an active debater. In 1902, he went on to King's College at Cambridge University, where he studied mainly mathematics and philosophy. He formed many of the enduring friendships of his life when he joined the Apostles, an intellectual society that held spirited discussions of philosophy and aesthetics. Eventually, Maynard's group of friends developed into a broader circle of unconventional writers, artists, and thinkers known as the Bloomsbury Group, which included the famous novelists Virginia Woolf and E. M. Forster.

For eight weeks of his final year at Cambridge, Maynard Keynes studied economics under classical economist Alfred Marshall. On Keynes's first paper for him, Marshall wrote, "I trust that your future career may be one in [which] you will not cease to be an economist." Despite this encouragement and the fact that he found the subject "easy and fascinating," Keynes did not continue his economic studies. Instead, he took the civil service exam and in 1907 went to work in the British government's India Office in London, writing his philosophy dissertation in his spare time. But he soon found himself "bored nine-tenths of the time and rather unreasonably irritated the other tenth," so on his 25th birthday he

Alfred Marshall (1842-1924) founded the economics department at Cambridge in 1902, around the time Keynes entered the university.

resigned from his job and returned to Cambridge as a lecturer in economics.

Keynes's academic career progressed rapidly. In 1909, his dissertation was accepted and he became a fellow of King's College. In 1911, with Alfred Marshall's backing, he was appointed editor of the leading economic publication of the time, the *Economic Journal*—a high honor for a 28-year-old economist. Keynes took great pride in his job, spending hours reviewing submissions before accepting or rejecting them for publication. Often he would write long notes, particularly for the young economists, providing reasons for his rejections and suggestions for improvement. The *Journal* also provided him with an outlet for publishing his own writing. Keynes retained the position for 34 years, overseeing 143 issues with a total of 1,100 articles.

The beginning of World War I in 1914 brought Keynes back to government employment, this time with the British Treasury. He moved to London, dividing his time between a frenzied social life of dancing and dinner parties and an exhausting workload at the Treasury. The nation faced a financial crisis, and Keynes was responsible for obtaining scarce foreign currency and external financing to pay for the British war effort. When the war ended, he traveled to Paris in January 1919 to represent the Treasury at the peace conference. He soon concluded that the victorious Allied nations were more interested in punishing Germany than negotiating a just and workable

The peace talks following World War I were held at the Ministry of Foreign Affairs in Paris.

treaty. Keynes believed that Great Britain and France were demanding excessive reparations (payments for damages sustained in war) from the defeated Germany. Frustrated and fatigued to the point of illness, he resigned before the conference ended with the signing of the Treaty of Versailles on June 28.

In December, he published his conclusions about the conference in *The Economic Consequences of the Peace*, a scorching critique of the treaty's terms. According to Keynes, the Allied leaders at the conference had acted from political motives, not economic ones. "The future life of Europe was not their concern; its means of livelihood was not their anxiety," he wrote. "Their preoccupations, good and bad alike, related to frontiers and nationalities, to the balance of power, to imperial aggrandisement, to the future enfeeblement of a strong and dangerous enemy, to revenge, and to the shifting by the victors of their unbearable financial burdens on to the shoulders of the defeated." Keynes calculated that Germany could not possibly meet the demands for reparations. The payments would shatter its postwar economy. Not only would this bring misery to thousands of Germans, but it also was hardly in the best interests of the Allied countries. The entire economy of Europe would be damaged, and Germany would remain an angry enemy.

Many of Keynes's predictions proved true. In the 1920s, a number of negotiations attempted to formulate workable reparations payments, for which the U.S. ultimately made loans to Germany. When American loans dried up during the Great Depression, Germany defaulted on its debts. Furthermore, the treaty fostered resentment and economic problems in Germany that helped pave the way for the rise of the Nazis and World War II.

The controversial *Economic Consequences of the Peace* brought Keynes worldwide fame. Over 100,000 copies were sold in the U.S. and Britain by July 1920, and the book was quickly translated into at least 11 other languages. Fresh from this success, Keynes next pursued a financial career in London. He managed an investment company, made a fortune speculating in international currencies and commodities, served as a director of several life insurance companies, became the bursar (treasurer) of King's College, helped manage the liberal journal *The Nation*, and continued writing on economic matters.

In 1925, Keynes married a Russian ballerina, Lydia Lopokova. The childless couple lived a happy existence, enjoying each other's company, going to parties, and attending theater and cultural events. They bought a farmhouse in East Sussex, where they vacationed. It was there, in an annex to the main house, that Keynes wrote

Keynes with Lydia Lopokova at their country home, Tilton, in 1928

his most theoretical works, *Treatise on Money* (1930) and *The General Theory of Employment, Interest and Money* (1936). *Treatise on Money* was not widely read, likely because the topic was narrow. But *The General Theory*, though a highly difficult and technical book, held so many fertile ideas that it revolutionized government economic policies.

The General Theory was essentially an analysis of the causes of unemployment, a particularly pressing problem during the economic depression of the 1930s. Keynes found that the classical economists—including his mentor, Alfred Marshall—were unable to explain the Great Depression. They believed that if there were goods available, consumers would always buy them, and thus there would be full employment to produce all the goods that people wanted. Employment, supply, or demand might fluctuate slightly, but the balance would always correct itself. In their theories, the long-term unemployment and reduced business activity of the Great Depression were impossible. Drawing on the century-old work of economist Thomas Robert Malthus, Keynes suggested that demand sometimes dropped below the level of production because people saved some of their income instead of spending it. If people spent less money on goods and services, businesses would fire workers and reduce production.

Classical economists argued that even if individuals saved more and consumed less, the economy would remain balanced because businesses would increase their investments. If people put more money into banks, it would be loaned to businesses, which would use the money to expand and create more jobs. But Keynes argued that when low consumer spending had already caused a recession, businesses might not want to expand if there was no demand for their products. Eventually, more workers would become unemployed and have no extra income to save. Therefore, no money would be available for businesses to borrow. The economy would become stagnant. Contrary to the belief of the classical economists, Keynes concluded, a depression might not cure itself.

Desperate to eat, hundreds of unemployed workers line up for a charity meal during the Depression.

Keynes believed that if businesses were unable to invest in the expansion needed to create jobs and boost consumer spending, then the government had to step in and fill this role. The government could inject money into the economy, spending funds on public programs that would create employment and put money in people's pockets. Keynes knew this idea would be opposed by those who believed that governments must avoid deficit spending (spending more than they collected from taxes). But he argued that trying to maintain a balanced budget in a depression was pointless. Since incomes had fallen, the government already took in less money in taxes. To balance the budget, it would have to cut spending or raise taxes, both of which would further damage the economy. If the government temporarily spent more to help the economy recover, then people's incomes would rise, more tax revenue would be generated, and the government would have enough money to pay off the deficit.

Keynes knew that increased government spending would be criticized by advocates of laissez-faire economics. But he saw the enlargement of government "as the only practicable means of avoiding the destruction of existing economic firms in their entirety and as the condition of the successful functioning of individual initiative." In other words, free-market capitalism could not operate if the economy was hopelessly stalled in a depression.

Keynes's theory provided a logical defense of recovery measures already being applied. Most significantly,

Keynes corresponded and met with President Franklin Roosevelt about a plan to pull the United States out of the Great Depression. Visiting the U.S. in 1934, just before finishing the first draft of *The General Theory*, he urged Roosevelt to expand his New Deal spending programs, which had begun in 1933. In addition to reform legislation, the New Deal consisted of many government relief programs that provided welfare and jobs, hiring millions of unemployed people to build roads and buildings, repair bridges, and set up community projects.

This political cartoon depicts President Roosevelt as a doctor trying to cure Uncle Sam's illness (the Great Depression). Each medicine bottle on the table is labeled with the name of a New Deal program.

Roosevelt was happy to find support for his experiment from an economist, but Keynes did not have an immediate influence on the president's actions. Roosevelt's main goal was simply to find jobs for people desperate to work. He did not resort to deficit spending and never expanded his programs as much as Keynes would have liked. In fact, he slashed the federal budget in 1937 and 1938, causing another economic slump. This time, the administration acted more directly on Keynes's ideas, using deficit spending to stimulate the economy. The "Roosevelt recession" passed. Keynes's theories seemed further proven when the Great Depression finally came to an end with World War II (1939-1945), a period of immense government spending.

Keynes's ideas launched an academic revolution in economics. It began with a circle of young Cambridge economists who met to discuss Keynes's *Treatise on Money* and then began commenting on drafts of *The General Theory* before it was published. Among the most notable was Richard Kahn (1905-1989), Keynes's favorite student, who supplied Keynes with the theory of the multiplier—the degree to which a spending change impacts economic activity. The multiplier meant that any individual change in spending started a chain reaction that affected the entire economy on a larger scale. Another important colleague, Joan Robinson (1903-1983), was instrumental in defending and expanding Keynes's ideas. In the U.S., the economics department of Harvard University became a stronghold of Keynesian beliefs. Soon, followers of Keynes had grown numerous enough to be referred to as the "Keynesian school" of economic thought. They explored in more detail the ways that governments could use spending and taxes to fine-tune the economy.

During World War II, Keynes advised the British Treasury and made several trips to the U.S. to discuss war finance. He had a major hand in shaping the postwar

This March 1940 newspaper article shows Keynes hard at work, formulating a plan to help Great Britain finance World War II.

Keynes (center) represents his country at a postwar economic conference.

economic system, leading the British delegation at the international monetary conference in Bretton Woods, New Hampshire, in 1944. The meeting established the International Monetary Fund, which promotes international monetary cooperation, currency stability, and trade expansion. It also created the World Bank, which provides loans to help developing economies improve their living standards and reduce poverty. Keynes performed his last major public service in 1945, when he negotiated a $3.75 billion loan from the United States to aid Britain's postwar recovery.

Throughout his life, Keynes was a man of varied interests. In addition to his many economic and political accomplishments, he served as a director of the Bank of England, a trustee of the National Gallery, and the chair of the newly formed Committee for the Encouragement of Music and the Arts, later called the British Arts Council. He collected antique books and modern art, and he built and managed a theater in Cambridge. He was even honored with the title of Lord Keynes, Baron of Tilton. But all this activity took a toll on his health, which began to decline in 1937, never to recover fully. On Easter Sunday, April 21, 1946, after suffering a series of heart attacks, John Maynard Keynes died at his home in Cambridge. He was just 63; both of his parents were still living.

Keynes defined his own legacy when he wrote, "The ideas of economists and political philosophers, both when they are right and when they are wrong, are more powerful than is commonly understood. Indeed the world is ruled by little else. Practical men, who believe themselves to be quite exempt from any intellectual influences, are usually the slaves of some defunct economist." From the 1930s to the early 1970s, the Keynesian school dominated economics with the belief that governments had a role in ensuring economic prosperity. This idea was reflected in legislation like the U.S. Employment Act of

1946, which proclaimed that it was the federal government's responsibility to "promote maximum employment, production, and purchasing power." World War II spending, big spending during the Vietnam War, and Lyndon Johnson's "Great Society" spending programs of 1964-1966 (which included Medicare, the Department of Housing and Urban Development, and more federal education funding) gave further proof of the power of Keynesian policies. "We are all Keynesians now," announced President Richard Nixon in 1971. Despite occasional recessions, the U.S. economy remained strong and unemployment low for several decades. Changing conditions in the 1970s prompted the rise of new economic theories that challenged the dominance of the Keynesian school, but some of its supporters still remained. Whether right or wrong, the ideas of Maynard Keynes forever changed the relationship between politics and economics, and the government policies they inspired continue to influence our lives today.

*In addition to creating a new school of economics,
Nobel Prize-winning economist Milton Friedman
(b. 1912) became a well-known public figure with his
controversial political views and his vocal opposition to
the theories of John Maynard Keynes.*

114

6

Milton Friedman
The Money Man

*M*ilton Friedman is definitely the money man. The titles of his books show his fascination: *The Optimum Quantity of Money and Other Essays* (1969); *Money Mischief: Episodes in Monetary History* (1992); and, coauthored with economist Anna Schwartz, *Monetary History of the United States, 1867-1960* (1963), *Monetary Statistics of the United States* (1970), and *Monetary Trends in the United States and the United Kingdom* (1982). Not surprisingly, Friedman is famous for inspiring a school of economics, called monetarism, that studies money and its effect on the economy.

The money man's beginnings were not graced by a great deal of money, but his upbringing was filled with support and love. On July 31, 1912, Milton Friedman was born in Brooklyn, New York. He was the last child of Sarah Ethel Landau Friedman and Jeno Saul Friedman, Jewish immigrants from what is now Ukraine, who already had three girls. When Milton was 13 months old, the family moved to Rahway, a small town in New Jersey. There his mother ran a dry goods store, which generated a modest income for the family to live on. Milton's father commuted to New York, where he worked in self-employed odd jobs that never earned much money. There were few luxuries in the household, but the notable exceptions were music lessons for the children. Although Milton found his violin lessons "a complete waste of time and money," they were a sign of the importance his parents placed on education.

Milton attended public elementary and secondary schools. He was a quick, eager learner, completing both sixth and seventh grades in a single year. He graduated from Rahway High School in 1928 with a good working knowledge of Latin, mathematics, and history. It was expected that Milton would have to finance his own college education, and his father's death during his senior year of high school made him even more determined to support himself. Luckily, the state of New Jersey had recently established competitive tuition scholarships to Rutgers University for students who could demonstrate need. Milton took the exam for the scholarship and was awarded financial assistance. He financed the rest of his educational expenses however he could, including clerking in a department store, waiting tables in exchange for lunches, selling socks and ties in the dormitories, and teaching summer school at Rahway High. In 1932, he graduated from Rutgers with a major in economics.

Milton went on to graduate study at the University of Chicago, where the economics department offered him a scholarship. It was there, in an economics theory course, that Milton met fellow graduate student Rose Director. The two became friends and were married in

Rose Director and Milton Friedman met when they ended up next to each other in an alphabetical seating arrangement in their Economics 301 class. "Our life [together] has surpassed our wildest expectations," they wrote 65 years later.

1938. They had a daughter, Janet, and a son, David. Rose would read and critique much of Milton's economic writings and become a partner in his public policy work.

After a year at Chicago, Milton Friedman was offered a substantial fellowship to Columbia University. He completed all the course studies at Columbia, then returned to Chicago to work as a research assistant to statistical economist Henry Schultz. In 1935, Friedman left academics temporarily to go to Washington, D.C., as part of President Franklin Roosevelt's New Deal (an assortment of government programs designed to end the Great Depression). He worked at the National Resources Committee on the design of a large consumer budget study, then moved to New York to work for the National Bureau of Economic Research. There, he assisted economist Simon Kuznets (who later won the Nobel Prize in economics) in studying income differences between professions. Their jointly published *Income from Independent Professional Practice* (1945) served as Friedman's doctoral thesis at Columbia, which awarded his Ph.D. in 1946.

When the United States entered World War II, Friedman returned to Washington to work on wartime tax policy at the U.S. Treasury Department. Next, he joined the Statistical Research Group at Columbia University as a statistician, working on problems like weapon design and military tactics. He found the research stimulating and enjoyed working with a wide spectrum of people, including scientists, engineers, and mathematicians.

Friedman spent a year teaching statistics and economics at the University of Minnesota before being offered a position on the University of Chicago faculty, where he remained for 30 years (1946-1976). It was at Chicago, surrounded by like-minded economists such as George J. Stigler (1982 Nobel Prize winner in economics), that Friedman did some of his most groundbreaking work in the study of money.

At the time, the field of economics was dominated by followers of John Maynard Keynes, who supported increased government spending to end economic depressions. Friedman, on the other hand, was a firm advocate of laissez-faire principles—no government interference

Friedman called the University of Chicago "a more stimulating intellectual environment . . . than any [I] have ever encountered elsewhere."

in the economy. Although he believed that government played a role in providing a stable legal and economic framework, he thought government spending should be based on the needs of the public, not on stimulating the economy. Trying to manage the economy would destabilize it, damage free-market competition, and make the situation worse. Throughout his career, Friedman sought to point out the limitations of Keynesian theory.

One of Friedman's first major economic ideas was his permanent income theory of consumption, introduced in *A Theory of the Consumption Function* (1957). Keynes had introduced the consumption function to predict how much the economy would swell or contract when the government adjusted its spending. In Keynes's theory, the consumption function was the relationship between spending and current income; people would spend less money when their incomes declined and more money when they rose. Friedman, however, building on his earlier work with professional incomes, suggested that people consumed not on current income, but on permanent income—the average of their lifetime income. For example, some people might be in a low-income group when they started their careers, but if they knew their earnings would increase soon, they would spend accordingly.

Although Friedman's theory was initially questioned, it was supported by later events. In 1968, for instance, the government passed a temporary tax increase to prevent inflation (rising prices), hoping that paying more money to the government would cause consumers to spend less on other things, which would make prices drop. But because they knew the extra tax was temporary and their incomes would rise again, consumers didn't change their standards of living; instead, they drew money out of savings to buy the things they wanted.

Because of the permanent income theory, Friedman concluded that temporary government policies (like tax increases or decreases) had only weak effects on the economy. What mattered, he said, was the amount of money in the economy. This was a direct challenge to Keynesian theory, which concentrated on fiscal policy (taxes and government spending, which are controlled in the United States by the presidential administration and Congress) and dismissed the role money played in the economy. Friedman and other monetarists, however, set out to examine the impact of monetary policy, which is largely controlled in the United States by the Federal Reserve Bank (the nation's central bank).

Monetarists based their ideas on the quantity theory of money, which says that when the money supply changes by a certain percentage, the price level will change by the same percentage. Although a lot of money seems like a good thing, money's value is measured by the amount of goods and services it can buy. If there is too much money trying to buy too few goods, the price of those goods will rise. Thus, according to the monetarists, too much money in the economy would cause inflation.

Friedman with students at the University of Chicago

On the other hand, too little money would cause a recession. Only a balance between the growth of money and the growth of production would keep the economy on a smooth course, providing the right amount of money to buy the goods produced, but not enough to raise prices.

When it was first introduced, monetarism was so different from the accepted economic theories that it was widely criticized or dismissed. But Friedman supported his ideas with historical studies that showed the power of money in the economy. In *Monetary History of the United States, 1867-1960*, Friedman and coauthor Anna Schwartz wrote that the Great Depression was "a tragic testament to the effectiveness of monetary policy, not a demonstration of its impotence." Keynesians believed that the money supply had expanded in the late 1920s and early 1930s, but that this had done nothing to prevent the economic crisis. Friedman and Schwartz found that between 1929 and 1933, the quantity of money in the economy had actually dropped by one-third. The Federal Reserve had not provided extra money to banks weakened by the 1929 stock market crash. Some banks did not have enough money to pay back customers who wanted to withdraw their savings, which caused people to panic and remove their money from banks, further shrinking the money supply. Friedman argued that this was a mistake in monetary policy and that similar mistakes had accompanied every significant recession and inflation in the past century. His careful presentation of evidence helped monetarism gain more acceptance in the 1960s and 1970s.

At that time, prices were anything but stable. Inflation and unemployment were high and production of goods and services was down, a situation labeled "stagflation" (a combination of "stagnation" and "inflation"). The majority of economists could not explain the situation. Keynesian theory maintained that there was a permanent tradeoff between inflation and unemployment: stimulating demand for goods and services would create more jobs to produce them but would make prices rise, while decreasing demand for goods and services would cause prices to fall but lead to more unemployment. But in the 1960s and 1970s, unemployment increased at the same time that prices rose. In a 1967 address to the American

Economic Association, Milton Friedman became the first to suggest that the tradeoff between inflation and unemployment was only temporary. He said there was a natural rate of unemployment—that no matter how strong the economy, there would always be a certain number of people who were unemployed (because, for instance, they were moving between jobs). Changes in demand or prices would have a temporary effect on unemployment, but eventually the economy would correct itself, returning to the natural rate of unemployment. Friedman explained that policymakers were trying to reduce unemployment below the natural rate, which only accelerated inflation: "A little inflation will produce a boost at first—like a small dose of a drug to a new addict—but then it takes more and more inflation to provide the boost, just as it takes a bigger and bigger dose of a drug to give a hardened addict a high." His analysis of the situation gained him further credit as an opponent of Keynesian theory.

By the 1980s, the inflation that had haunted the U.S. for a decade had reached a rate high enough for the monetarists' point to be taken seriously by both academics and the government. At President Ronald Reagan's urging, Federal Reserve Chairman Paul Volcker announced that he would begin reducing the growth of the money supply to cut inflation. The road back to stability was not easy, however. The economy weathered two recessions in the early 1980s, interest rates fluctuated wildly, and unemployment rose to more than 10 percent. But inflation plummeted, falling from over 12 percent in 1980 to less than 4 percent in 1982, and it remained stable for the remainder of the decade. Although Friedman personally opposed government manipulation of the money supply, the Federal Reserve's action had proven his theory that the amount of money in the economy affected inflation. Central banks in countries throughout the world began monitoring the supply of money in their economies. Monetarism had found its way into mainstream economics.

In addition to his academic work, Friedman wrote and published extensively—and often controversially—on public policy. At a time when it was unusual for professional economists to involve themselves directly in political arguments, he argued tirelessly for limited government and individual freedom. His specific positions were, as he described them, "opposition to rent control and general wage and price controls, . . . support for educational choice, privatizing radio and television channels, an all-volunteer army, limitation of government spending, legalization of drugs, privatizing social security, free trade, and the deregulation of industry and private life to the fullest extent possible." Friedman presented some of these ideas in a collection of lectures called *Capitalism and Freedom* (1962). The book, along with the 300 economic columns Friedman wrote for *Newsweek* from 1966 to 1984, turned him into a well-known public figure and gained him both supporters and critics. He found writing for a wide audience "challenging and highly rewarding. It has forced me to try . . . to express technical economics in language accessible to all. . . . I have learned in the process how easy it is to be misunderstood or—to say the same thing—how hard it is to be crystal clear. I have learned also how numerous are the perspectives from which any issue can be viewed. There is no such thing as a purely economic issue."

Friedman continued reaching a broad audience with his 10-part television series, *Free to Choose*, which aired on public television (PBS) from January to March 1980 and attracted an average of three million viewers—outstanding for PBS at the time. Friedman called the filming of *Free to Choose* his most memorable working experience, "because it was altogether different from anything I had ever done. I had done pieces on television, but they were all isolated talks or participation in a discussion. I had never been involved in developing a lengthy documentary. . . . We traveled all over the world in filming, filmed under all sorts of different circumstances, met with a wide variety of different people." The money man "got a real kick out of" filming money being printed at the U.S. Bureau of Engraving and Printing in Washington, D.C., and another scene was filmed in the gold vaults of the Federal Reserve Bank of New York with Friedman "giving a little bit of a talk while seated on a bench of solid gold." In early 1984, Friedman followed up the series with another, called *Tyranny of the Status Quo*. He and his wife, Rose, also cowrote books to complement both PBS series.

Friedman's publications, awards, and appointments are almost too numerous to detail. He was granted 19 honorary degrees from universities in the U.S. and abroad. He served as president of the American Economic Association in 1967. In 1976, he received the Nobel Prize in economic science—for his work in monetary history and theory, consumption analysis, and the practical application of economics. Friedman was also awarded both the National Medal of Science and the Presidential Medal of Freedom (the nation's highest civilian award) in 1988.

Milton Friedman accepts the Nobel Prize medal and certificate from King Carl XVI of Sweden.

Ronald Reagan (with Nancy Reagan) gives Friedman the Presidential Medal of Freedom. Friedman enjoyed a good relationship with President Reagan, who shared many of his economic and political beliefs.

Friedman worked as economic adviser to conservative Republican senator Barry Goldwater in his unsuccessful bid for the 1964 presidency. He then advised Richard Nixon and Ronald Reagan during their victorious presidential campaigns and in their administrations.

After Friedman retired from active teaching at the University of Chicago in 1976, he worked as a senior research fellow at the Hoover Institution (a research center dedicated to the study of politics, economics, and international affairs) at Stanford University. He also continued to write, and in 1998 he and Rose published *Two*

Lucky People, a memoir of their successful marriage and rewarding professional careers. In 1996, the Friedmans established the Milton & Rose D. Friedman Foundation, a nonprofit organization that promotes education reform.

Despite Friedman's success at bringing his unorthodox economic ideas into the mainstream, the United States has not continued to follow a monetarist path. Since late 1982, the Federal Reserve has guided the economy largely through interest rates, not directly through the money supply. This highlights an important point in economics: no economic school or philosophy is perfectly applicable to all economies at all times. Theories have their heydays, and monetarism won many devotees in the 1970s and 1980s. But policymakers, government officials, and business leaders take bits and pieces of many theories to help guide their economies.

Economists can no longer be divided strictly into Keynesians and monetarists, since both groups have introduced theories that are widely accepted. Monetarism's major contribution was convincing economists that the growth rate of the money supply has consequences for the economy. Of the results of his theories, Friedman has said, "Almost all economists—whether they label themselves Keynesians, monetarists, rational expectationists, or believers in a real business cycle—recognize that money does matter, that what happens to the quantity of money has important effects on economic activity in the short run and on the price level in the long run."

With an approach to economics that has been described as "putting Keynes's head on Milton Friedman's body," Alan Greenspan (b. 1926) successfully guided the Federal Reserve for more than 15 years.

7

Alan Greenspan
Federal Reserve Chairman

*I*n 1987, when Paul Volcker told President Ronald Reagan that he would not serve another term as Federal Reserve chairman, Alan Greenspan's name was on the shortlist to replace him. Greenspan, a Republican with a conservative economic philosophy, had held political appointments that included acting as an economic adviser during Reagan's campaign and chairing a commission on Social Security reform. On June 1, 1987, President Reagan called Greenspan to ask him if he would accept the Federal Reserve chairmanship. Greenspan, however, was at the doctor's office being treated for his bad back. It took about 20 minutes to locate him before he quickly said yes. Greenspan's presidential nomination was confirmed by a Senate vote of 91 to 2. He dissolved his New York consulting company, Townsend-Greenspan, and was off to Washington, D.C. On August 11, Alan Greenspan became chairman of the most powerful central bank in the world. His life would never be the same.

Alan Greenspan was born on March 6, 1926, in New York City. He was the only child of Herbert Greenspan, a stockbroker, and Rose Goldsmith Greenspan. When Alan was just five years old, his parents divorced; he rarely saw his father after the breakup. Rose and Alan moved in with her parents in a one-bedroom apartment in the Washington Heights neighborhood of Manhattan.

Alan showed remarkable signs of early intelligence. By the age of five, he could add three-digit numbers and solve mathematical puzzles in his head. He excelled in school, completing seventh, eighth, and ninth grades in a total of just two years. Inheriting a love of music from his mother, Alan learned to play the clarinet and the saxophone. He played in the school orchestra and in a band that performed at school dances, and he hoped to become a professional musician someday.

After graduating from George Washington High School in 1943, Alan went on to study music at the prestigious Juilliard School. Restless, he dropped out of Juilliard after a few months and joined a touring swing band, Henry Jerome and His Orchestra. But as his fellow band members were living it up on the road, Alan Greenspan found himself keeping track of the band's finances and helping other musicians with their taxes. During breaks in his performances, he read economics books borrowed from local libraries. When he discovered that his love of math gave him a natural aptitude for the study of economics, Alan Greenspan found his calling.

At the age of 19, Greenspan left the band and enrolled at New York University. He earned a bachelor's degree in economics in 1948 and his master's in economics in 1950. Greenspan then began advanced graduate work at Columbia University, where he studied under famed economist Arthur F. Burns. Burns would be not only a teacher to Greenspan, but also his predecessor as Federal Reserve chairman (1970-1978) and a lifelong mentor. Burns was one of the few economists at the time who disagreed with John Maynard Keynes's theory that government spending was needed to stimulate the economy in times of depression. Burns believed in the natural business cycle—that the economy would correct itself without the government intervention Keynes advocated. From Burns, Greenspan developed the belief that excess government spending could lead to inflation, and that businesses should be allowed to compete without government interference.

Unable to afford tuition, Greenspan eventually dropped out of Columbia to work for an economic research group called the National Industrial Conference Board. (He did return to New York University to work on his Ph.D. on and off over several decades, finally earning the degree in 1977.) In 1954, Greenspan joined with bond trader William Townsend to form an economic consulting firm, Townsend-Greenspan, in New York City. Older and more experienced, Townsend acted as president while Greenspan served as the vice president. When Townsend died in 1958, Greenspan took over the running of the firm as its president. He guided the company to heightened prosperity, becoming a millionaire by the late 1960s. Compiling economic data and forecasting trends for some of the nation's biggest banks and manufacturing companies was excellent training for the future Federal Reserve chairman, who would need familiarity with large amounts of data and all levels of the U.S. economy.

Greenspan married artist Joan Mitchell in 1952, but the marriage lasted only 10 months. They remained friends, however, and it was Mitchell who introduced Greenspan to the philosopher and novelist Ayn Rand. Rand had developed a philosophy called Objectivism, which—among other things—promoted free-market capitalism without government interference. Greenspan delved into Rand's unconventional ideas and spent hours discussing economics and other issues with Rand and her inner circle. As the years went by, Greenspan would see less and less of Rand, but their friendship endured until her death in 1982.

Ayn Rand (1905-1982) was most famous for her novels The Fountainhead *(1943) and* Atlas Shrugged *(1957). In these and in her philosophical teachings, she promoted rationality, self-interest, and competition.*

It was at Rand's urging that Greenspan first entered politics in 1968, as director of domestic policy research for Richard Nixon's presidential campaign. After winning, Nixon offered Greenspan a position as budget director in the administration. Greenspan declined, opting to return to his consulting firm, though he stayed active in Washington as an informal adviser on a variety of economic task forces. Then in 1974, during Nixon's second term, Greenspan was asked to be chairman of the President's Council of Economic Advisers. His mentor Arthur Burns, now Federal Reserve chairman, urged him to take the job to help combat the rising inflation that was

135

hurting the economy. Greenspan accepted, although by the time he took office in September 1974, Nixon had already resigned and been replaced by Gerald Ford. The inflationary mid-1970s were tough times to be in a position of economic power, but Greenspan influenced policies to restrain government spending and helped dampen inflation. After Ford, a Republican, was defeated by Democrat Jimmy Carter in the 1976 election, Greenspan returned to New York and Townsend-Greenspan.

Gerald Ford (right) valued Greenspan's economic advice. Dick Cheney, Ford's chief of staff, observed: "At the end of the day, after he talked to everybody else, President Ford would say, 'Let's get Alan over here,' and then Ford would make the key decision."

By the turn of the 1980s, the United States economy was struggling. The country experienced a brief recession, or downturn in business activity, in early 1980. Then, in mid-1981, the country fell into a deeper recession that persisted for 16 months. In the midst of all this economic turmoil, Ronald Reagan began his presidency. In addition to high inflation, high unemployment, and high interest rates, Reagan had inherited problems with Social Security (a government fund to assist the unemployed, disabled, and elderly). Escalating inflation had seriously crippled the system, which soon would be unable to pay full benefit checks to retirees. The Reagan administration asked Greenspan to chair the 15-member National Commission on Social Security Reform to address the problem.

Greenspan's influence was so great that the commission, which lasted from 1981 to 1983, became known as the Greenspan Commission. He impressed Reagan by developing a plan that temporarily put Social Security back on sound footing, taxing benefit payments and increasing the amount deducted from workers' paychecks for the fund. Reagan responded by nominating Greenspan as Federal Reserve chairman.

The Federal Reserve (known as "the Fed") is the central bank of the United States. It controls monetary policy—how much money is in circulation and how easily it can be borrowed. The Fed is independent of Congress and the president's administration, which control fiscal policy—taxes and government spending. When he

Days after being nominated as the new Federal Reserve chairman, Greenspan shakes hands with Ronald Reagan at the White House; outgoing Fed Chairman Paul Volcker (behind and to the left) looks on.

assumed the Fed chairmanship in 1987, Greenspan became the head of two committees: the seven-member Board of Governors and the twelve-member Federal Open Market Committee (FOMC). The FOMC, made up of the seven members of the Board of Governors plus five Federal Reserve bank presidents, is the real power-house behind the economy. It is in charge of open market operations, or buying and selling government bonds, for the Fed. When the Fed buys bonds, it expands the money supply, giving banks more money to lend. When banks have more money, they are willing to lend it more cheaply, and interest rates (the amount of money banks charge on loans) fall. On the other hand, when the Fed sells bonds, it reduces the amount of money in circulation and interest rates rise.

The rising and falling of interest rates affects the economy. By discouraging people and businesses from borrowing—and thus spending—money, high interest rates slow down the economy and can cause a recession.

Federal Reserve headquarters in Washington, D.C.

Low interest rates make loans easier to get, allowing businesses to expand and create more jobs, while encouraging individuals to buy homes and spend more money on consumer items. But a large amount of economic growth can lead to inflation. Higher prices for goods and services cause people and businesses to stop spending money, triggering a recession. The Fed tries to make sure that the economy grows, but also tries to keep it from growing dangerously fast. The FOMC guides the economy's path by meeting eight times each year to set the direction for monetary policy—deciding if interest rates should rise,

A meeting of the Federal Open Market Committee at the Fed headquarters

fall, or remain the same. Everyone concerned with the state of the economy—including businesspeople, politicians, and average citizens—watches the chairman, the most influential member of the committee, for hints about the future course of interest rates.

Greenspan had only been Fed chair for two months when a major financial emergency hit the United States. On Monday, October 19, 1987 (a day that came to be called "Black Monday"), the stock market's Dow Jones Industrial Average plunged 508 points. American investors lost $500 billion, and overseas markets plummeted, too. The stock market drop was almost twice as big as the one in 1929 that had helped launch the Great Depression. At that time, banks had made the situation worse by reducing their lending. To avert a similar disaster in 1987, Greenspan calmed the banks by stating that the Fed was prepared to pump money into the economy as needed. Greenspan's mere willingness to provide money was just what the public wanted to hear, and stocks quickly rebounded. In two weeks, the economy stabilized. Alan Greenspan had worked his magic.

Greenspan accomplished much of his important daily data analysis while soaking in the bathtub to relieve his back pain. The monetary policy that emerged from these early-morning soaks was squarely aimed at targeting inflation rates. Greenspan sought to fight inflation while maintaining solid employment and production levels. Whenever he thought the economy was going too strong and inflation might rear its ugly head—most notoriously in 1988-1989 and 1994-1995—he hiked interest rates. These widely unpopular, though effective, moves won Greenspan the label of "inflation hawk."

Greenspan's campaign against inflation led to a troubled relationship with President George H. W. Bush's administration (1989-1993). Although the Fed is supposed to be independent of the president's influence, Bush wanted Greenspan to lower the interest rates to spur economic growth. When Greenspan, guarding against inflation, did not do so, Bush publicly criticized him. In the summer of 1991, Bush renominated Greenspan for a

George Bush's repeated demands that "interest rates should be lower—now" led to tension with Alan Greenspan.

second four-year term, apparently because he could not find an adequate replacement. But when Bush lost the 1992 election to Bill Clinton, he blamed Greenspan for the defeat: "I think that if the interest rates had been lowered more dramatically that I would have been reelected president because the [economic] recovery that we were in would have been more visible. I reappointed him, and he disappointed me."

Surprisingly to some, Greenspan got along much better with Bill Clinton's Democratic administration (1993-2001). President Clinton renominated Greenspan for a third term, which began in June 1996. The Fed chairman continued trying to keep the economy running somewhere between full-force and a snail's pace. And, by almost unanimous accounts, he did so very astutely. In fact, Greenspan proved to have a magic touch when it came to guiding the economy. The 1990s brought only one mild, short-lived recession, from mid-1990 to early 1991. Throughout the rest of the decade, the U.S. experienced its longest expansion period in history: strong production of goods and services, high employment, modest inflation, and huge stock market gains. Although the boom eventually slowed, Greenspan became so closely associated with this unparalleled economic growth and success that he became a pop-culture celebrity.

A few brief words from Greenspan could make the stock market skyrocket or dive tumultuously. The strongest example of the power of his words was his now-famous "irrational exuberance" speech. On the evening of December 5, 1996, Greenspan gave a speech entitled "The Challenge of Central Banking in a Democratic Society" while accepting an award from The American Enterprise Institute for Public Policy Research. Halfway through the talk he happened to pose the question, "But how do we know when irrational exuberance has unduly escalated asset values?" The media covering the event picked up on the question. When financial traders around the world heard Greenspan's words, they thought he was saying that stock prices were overvalued. Although the U.S. market was closed for the day, other world markets were open, and the global selloff in stocks began. When the U.S. market opened the next morning, the Dow Jones Industrial Average fell 145.35 points within the first half-hour of trading. Whether Greenspan wanted to send a signal that stock prices were too high is a matter of debate, but the event was a clear sign of how closely the economy took its cue from him.

To avoid sending unintentional messages, Greenspan became a master of speaking ambiguously. (Once, when testifying before Congress, he told them, "I know you understand what you think I said, but I am not sure you realize that what you heard is not what I said.") But Fed watchers found other ways to monitor Greenspan's opinion of the economy. The CNBC news network even came up with a tongue-in-cheek economic signpost called the "briefcase indicator." Reported each time the FOMC met to set the direction for the nation's money supply, the briefcase indicator was supposed to predict whether interest rates would change. Supposedly, if Greenspan's closely guarded briefcase was thick when he arrived at the meeting, he had been doing a lot of research and needed the documentation to convince other members of the FOMC of the need to change interest rates. If the briefcase was thin, interest rates would stay the same. According to CNBC, the briefcase indicator was correct 19 of the first 20 times it was reported.

Greenspan works hard to analyze and shape the economic climate. "That crazy economy out there doesn't stand still long enough for us to get a fix on it," he once said. "It continually changes too rapidly for us to apply our techniques."

Greenspan's personal life was as successful as his career. In 1997, after dating NBC political correspondent Andrea Mitchell for about 12 years, he married her in a ceremony conducted by Supreme Court Justice Ruth Bader Ginsburg. In addition to his work at the Fed, Greenspan accumulated a staggering list of honors, awards, and appointments. Among the most notable were his positions as a member of *Time* magazine's board of economists, a senior adviser to the Brookings Panel on Economic Activity, and President and Fellow of the National Association of Business Economists. Greenspan received honorary degrees from seven universities, including Harvard, Yale, and Notre Dame.

Nominated again by President Clinton, Greenspan began serving his fourth and final term as Fed chairman on June 20, 2000. At the Senate hearings on his renomination, Greenspan expressed his love of the job: "It has been an extraordinary privilege to be able to serve my country at the Federal Reserve, and I would be honored if the Senate saw fit to continue this association for another four years."

After a decade of prosperity, Greenspan faced a new challenge as U.S. economic growth began to slow in 2001. The situation worsened when, on September 11 of that year, terrorist attacks on the World Trade Center in New York City and the Pentagon in Washington, D.C., nearly halted economic activity and severely shook consumer confidence. Wall Street shut down for several days, and when it reopened, stocks plummeted. It became clear the country was now in a full-blown recession, and Greenspan acted quickly to handle the crisis. As it had after the 1987 stock market crash, the Fed promised to supply funds to the banking system so that banks would have enough money to deal with emergency withdrawals and continue making loans. The Fed slashed interest rates to the lowest level in 40 years, and Greenspan counseled President George W. Bush and Congress on plans to stimulate the economy.

By March 2002, Greenspan was announcing that the recession seemed to have ended and that "economic expansion is already underway." Although it remained to be seen how long it would take for the country to rebound completely, many observers concluded that the Fed chairman had triumphed again. Alan Greenspan retained his firm faith in the strong economy he had devoted so many years to nurturing. "The foundations of our free society remain sound," he said. "And I am confident that we will recover and prosper, as we have in the past."

Glossary of Economic Terms

barter: to exchange goods for other goods, without the use of money

capital: wealth produced by capitalism, usually in the form of money, property, or goods that produce income

capitalism: an economic system based on private property, individual action, and free-market competition

classical economics: a school of economics inspired by Adam Smith's analysis of free-market capitalism, promoting a laissez-faire approach to the economy

communism: an economic system based on public ownership of property and abolition of class differences

depression: a period of drastic economic decline

economist: a person who studies the way in which individuals and societies use their resources to produce, distribute, and consume goods and services

exchange rate: the value of a nation's currency in relation to other currencies

export: to ship goods abroad for trade or sale

Federal Reserve Bank ("Fed"): the central bank of the United States

fiscal policy: a course of action related to taxes and government spending, controlled in the United States by the presidential administration and Congress

guild: an organization of merchants or craftspeople grouped together to protect themselves from competition

import: to bring in goods from a foreign country for trade or sale

inflation: a rise in prices or decline in the purchasing power of money, caused by too much money or credit being available to buy existing goods and services

interest: money charged on a loan, usually a percentage of the amount loaned

Keynesian economics: a school of economics that believes government intervention is the best method for ensuring economic growth and stability

laissez-faire: the belief that the economy functions best when free from government control; French for "allow to do"

mercantilism: an economic system in which monarchs strictly controlled economic activity to accumulate more wealth

monetarism: a school of economics that studies money and its effect on the economy

monetary policy: a course of action related to how much money is in circulation and how easily it can be borrowed, controlled in the United States by the Federal Reserve Bank

monopoly: a business interest that has exclusive control over production or sales of a good or service

recession: a temporary decline in business activity

tariff: a tax on goods entering or leaving a country

Bibliography

Beckner, Steven K. *Back from the Brink: The Greenspan Years.* New York: Wiley, 1996.

Blumenberg, Werner. *Karl Marx: An Illustrated Biography.* London: Verso, 1998.

Bonar, James. *Malthus and His Work.* London: Cass, 1966.

Buchholtz, Todd G. *New Ideas from Dead Economists: An Introduction to Modern Economic Thought.* 2nd ed. New York: Penguin, 1999.

Burgon, John William. *The Life and Times of Sir Thomas Gresham, Founder of the Royal Exchange.* London: Charles Knight, 1845.

Butler, Eamonn. *Milton Friedman: A Guide to His Economic Thought.* New York: Universe, 1985.

Colander, David C. *Macroeconomics.* Chicago: Irwin, 1995.

Eatwell, John, Murray Milgate, and Peter Newman, eds. *The New Palgrave: A Dictionary of Economics.* London: Macmillan, 1988.

Federal Reserve Board. "Alan Greenspan." www.federalreserve.gov/bios/Greenspan.htm, cited October 3, 2000.

Flynn, John T. *Men of Wealth: The Story of Twelve Significant Fortunes from the Renaissance to the Present Day.* New York: Simon & Schuster, 1941.

Friedman, Milton. *Capitalism and Freedom.* Chicago: University of Chicago Press, 1982.

———. Letter to author, January 22, 2001.

———. *Money Mischief: Episodes in Monetary History.* San Diego: Harcourt Brace Jovanovich, 1992.

————. *Why Government is the Problem* (Essays in Public Policy No. 39). Stanford: Hoover Institution, Stanford University, 1993.

Friedman, Milton and Rose D. *Two Lucky People: Memoirs.* Chicago: University of Chicago Press, 1998.

————. *Tyranny of the Status Quo.* San Diego: Harcourt Brace Jovanovich, 1984.

Glass, D. V., ed. *Introduction to Malthus.* London: Watts, 1953.

Greenspan, Alan. "The Challenge of Central Banking in a Democratic Society." Speech presented at the Annual Dinner and Francis Boyer Lecture of The American Enterprise Institute for Public Policy Research, Washington, D.C., December 5, 1996. www.federalreserve.gov/boarddocs/speeches/1996/ 19961205.htm, cited January 21, 2002.

————. "Rules vs. Discretionary Monetary Policy." Speech presented at the 15th Anniversary Conference of the Center for Economic Policy Research at Stanford University, California, September 5, 1997. www.federalreserve.gov/boarddocs/speeches/1997/ 19970905.htm, cited January 21, 2002.

————. Testimony on the condition of the financial markets, presented before the Committee on Banking, Housing, and Urban Affairs, U.S. Senate, Setember 20, 2001. www.federalreserve.gov/boarddocs/testimony/2001/ 20010920.htm, cited April 1, 2002.

————. Testimony on nomination to fourth term as Chairman, presented before the Committee on Banking, Housing, and Urban Affairs, U.S. Senate, January 26, 2000. www.federalreserve.gov/boarddocs/testimony/2000/ 20000126.htm, cited January 21, 2002.

Gresham, Perry Epler. *The Sign of the Golden Grasshopper: A Biography of Sir Thomas Gresham.* Ottawa, Ill.: Jameson, 1995.

Griffith, G. Talbot. *Population Problems of the Age of Malthus.* London: Cambridge University Press, 1925.

Harrod, R. F. *The Life of John Maynard Keynes.* London: Macmillan, 1951.

Heilbroner, Robert L. *The Worldly Philosophers: The Lives, Times, and Ideas of the Great Economic Thinkers.* New York: Simon & Schuster, 1999.

Lekachman, Robert. *The Age of Keynes.* New York: Random House, 1966.

McConnell, John W. *The Basic Teachings of the Great Economists.* New York: New Home Library, 1943.

Mai, Ludwig H. *Men and Ideas in Economics: A Dictionary of World Economists Past and Present.* Totowa, N.J.: Littlefield, Adams, 1975.

Malthus, Thomas Robert. *An Essay on the Principle of Population* (1798). Ed. Philip Appleman. New York: Norton, 1976.

Martin, Justin. *Greenspan: The Man Behind Money.* Cambridge, Mass.: Perseus, 2000.

Marx, Karl. *Capital* (1876). Ed. Friedrich Engels. Chicago: Encyclopedia Britannica, 1952.

Marx, Karl, and Friedrich Engels. *The Communist Manifesto* (1888). New York: Bantam, 1992.

Marx and Engels Internet Archive. www.marxists.org/archive/marx/index.htm, cited January 21, 2002.

The Mercers' Company website. www.mercers.co.uk, cited November 12, 2000.

Moggridge, D. E. *Maynard Keynes: An Economist's Biography.* London: Routledge, 1992.

Nickerson, Jane Soames. *Homage to Malthus.* Port Washington, N.Y.: Kennikat, 1975.

Petersen, William. *Founder of Modern Demography: Malthus.* New Brunswick, N.J.: Transaction, 1999.

———. *Malthus.* Cambridge, Mass.: Harvard University Press, 1979.

Pirie, Madsen. Interview by author, November 2000.

Pressman, Steven. *Fifty Major Economists.* London: Routledge, 1999.

Raphael, D. D., Donald Winch, and Robert Skidelsky. *Three Great Economists: Smith, Malthus, Keynes.* Oxford: Oxford University Press, 1997.

Ross, Ian Simpson. *The Life of Adam Smith.* Oxford: Oxford University Press, 1995.

Selfridge, H. Gordon. *The Romance of Commerce.* London: John Lane, The Bodley Head, 1918.

Skidelsky, Robert. *John Maynard Keynes: Hopes Betrayed, 1883-1920.* New York: Penguin, 1983.

Slavin, Steve. *Economics: A Self-Teaching Guide.* New York: Wiley, 1999.

Smith, Adam. *The Theory of Moral Sentiments* (1759). Amherst, N.Y.: Prometheus, 2000.

———. *The Wealth of Nations* (1776). Amherst, N.Y.: Prometheus, 1991.

Soule, George. *Ideas of the Great Economists.* New York: Viking, 1952.

Spargo, John. *Karl Marx: His Life and Work.* New York: B. W. Huebsch, 1910.

West, E. G. *Adam Smith: The Man and His Works.* New Rochelle, N.Y.: Arlington House, 1969.

Wheen, Francis. *Karl Marx: A Life.* New York: Norton, 1999.

Woodward, Bob. *Maestro: Greenspan's Fed and the American Boom.* New York: Simon & Schuster, 2000.

Index

155

advocate of free trade, 36, 48-49, 51, 53; death of, 53; early years of, 39; education of, 39, 41-42; friendship of, with Hume, 43, 44, 45, 50; influence of, 15, 37, 38, 50-51, 54-55; personality of, 37-38, 45, 53; as teacher and tutor, 43, 44-45, 46; and theory of capitalism, 13, 36, 46-48, 53, 54; *Wealth of Nations* written by, 36, 46-47, 49, 50-51, 53, 55, 72
Smith, Adam (father), 38-39
Smith, Hugh (half-brother), 38
Smith, Margaret Douglas (mother), 39, 42, 53
Social Security, 131, 137
Somerset, duke of, 26
stagflation, 123
Stanford University, 128
Stigler, George J., 119
stock market, 143-144, 147; 1929 crash of, 15, 97, 123, 141; 1987 crash of, 141, 147
supply and demand, 13, 54, 72, 105

tariffs, 48-49, 51, 53
taxes, 12, 24, 48, 50, 53, 107, 120-121, 127
The Theory of Moral Sentiments, 43, 45
A Theory of the Consumption Function, 120
Townsend, William, 134
Townsend-Greenspan, 132, 134, 135, 136
Townshend, Charles, 43-44
trade, 8-9, 10, 11, 12-13, 17, 19, 20, 34
trading companies, 48, 54
Treasury, U.S., 6, 118
A Treatise of Human Nature, 41
Treatise on Money, 105, 109

Two Lucky People, 128-129
Tyranny of the Status Quo, 126

unemployment, 7, 97, 105-106, 113, 123-124, 137
utopia, 63, 65

Versailles, Treaty of, 102
Vietnam War, 113
Volcker, Paul, 124, 131, 138
Voltaire, 45

The Wealth of Nations. See *An Inquiry into the Nature and Causes of the Wealth of Nations*
Woolf, Virginia, 99
working conditions in factories, 13-14, 54, 63, 77, 83, 91, 93
World Bank, 111
World War I, 94, 101, 102
World War II, 15, 103, 109, 110, 113, 118

Young Hegelians, 80-81

159

ABOUT THE AUTHOR

MARIE BUSSING-BURKS holds an MBA and a doctorate in economics and has taught the discipline for 12 years at the University of Southern Indiana. She is the author of 3 books, including *Profit from the Evening News* (2001), and 30 magazine, newspaper, and journal articles in the field of economics and finance. Her work has appeared in such publications as *Health & Money*, *The American Economist*, and *College Teaching*. Bussing-Burks lives in Newburgh, Indiana, with her family.

Photo Credits

Photographs courtesy of: cover (top), pp. 114, 122, Special Collections Research Center, University of Chicago; cover (bottom), pp. 130, 139, 140, Federal Reserve; p. 6, National Archives; pp. 10, 26, 28, 30, 36, 51, 56, 71, 73, 106, 119, 135, Library of Congress; pp. 12, 14, 24, 62, 67, 69, 95, 96, 102, 108, 110, 111, Hulton/Archive by Getty Images; pp. 18, 22, 32, 35, the Mercers' Company; pp. 40 (both), 42, 47, 49, 52, Glasgow University Library, Department of Special Collections; p. 44, Scottish National Portrait Gallery; pp. 59, 60, Surrey History Centre; pp. 61, 64, Master and Fellows of Jesus College, Cambridge; pp. 76, 79, 81, 84, 86, 88, 90, 92, back cover, Studienzentrum Karl-Marx-Haus Trier; pp. 99, 104, Dr. Milo Keynes; p. 100, University of Cambridge, Faculty of Economics and Politics; pp. 117, 127, Milton and Rose Friedman; pp. 128, 138, Ronald Reagan Library; pp. 136, 145, Gerald R. Ford Library; p. 142, George Bush Presidential Library.